One of the most important books of the year: brutally honest, jaw-droopingly perceptive, yet unwaveringly hopeful. Sayers is an evil genius. I literally could not put this book down. A must read for every Christian in the West.

— **JOHN MARK COMER,** pastor for vision and teaching at Bridgetown Church in Portland, OR, author of *Loveology*

There are very few writers I read with more anticipation and astonishment than Mark Sayers. In this wide-ranging book, he offers the most concise, acute diagnosis I've seen of the predicament of the church in the "third culture" of neo-Gnostic post-Christendom—and kindles hope that this could still be one of the church's finest hours.

—**ANDY CROUCH,** executive editor, *Christianity Today* and author, *Culture Making: Recovering our Creative Calling* and *Playing God: Redeeming the Gift of Power*

Mark has given us a culturally astute, philosophically keen handbook to navigate challenges facing the Western church. Some passages are so loaded with insight I gladly read and reread them. Required, engaging reading for anyone serious about the faith.

—**JONATHAN DODSON,** lead pastor of City Life Church, author of *The Unbelievable Gospel* and *Raised? Finding Jesus by Doubting the Resurrection*

Brilliantly insightful, Sayers takes us beyond the obvious and shows us the deeper devotions of the contemporary self drunk on autonomy and resistant to the Christian faith. *Disappearing Church* is a prophetic call to gospel resilience, challenging the church's anemic attempts at relevance while inspiring a new posture in discipleship and mission. This is Sayers at his best.

—**JR VASSAR,** lead pastor, Church at the Cross and author of *Glory Hunger: God the Gospel and Our Quest for Something More*

There's not a keener observer of church and culture trends than Mark Sayers. And *Disappearing Church* comes at the perfect time, just as Western Christians are debating how best to navigate a rapidly secularizing culture. I can't imagine a more timely or important book.

—**DREW DYCK,** senior editor of *Leadership Journal* and author of *Generation Ex-Christian* and *Yawning at Tigers*

Disappearing Church is essential reading for those looking for how to be a compelling and faithful counterculture in these complex and challenging times. Mark has an incredible ability to deconstruct our current moment, but also construct a picture of how the church can bear witness to the way of Jesus and the good news of the gospel in this heavily contested world.

—**JON TYSON,** founding pastor of Trinity Grace Church New York, author of *Sacred Roots*

When Mark Sayers writes something I want to read it and pay attention. He is one of the rare people who can take deep thinking and insights and make them practical.

—**DAN KIMBALL**, Vintage Faith Church, director of the Regeneration project at Western Seminary, author of *They Like Jesus but Not the Church*

If you are ready to think rather than be thought to, ready to journey rather than be told, then prepare yourself to see our current reality from the inside out. In *Disappearing Church*, Mark Sayers helps us understand our current experience as the church in the West by taking us past the soft facades onto the hard truths while getting us back on track to the joy of the kingdom of heaven.

—**LANCE FORD**, author of *Revangelical*

Disappearing Church is a powerful look at the church's current state, how we got here, and what it will take to move past "relevance" into actually impacting the world. It is brilliantly crafted and deep while also being accessible and enjoyable. I always benefit when I read Mark's work, and this book is no exception.

—**BARNABAS PIPER**, author and podcaster

Mark Sayers traces how the church has tried to stay relevant in a changing world and nearly lost her soul in the process. With a balanced blend of history, theology, and cultural exegesis Mark proposes a hopeful vision for the church that is less about catering to public opinion and more about learning to live out and preach the gospel with courage and humility as a creative minority.

—**KEN WYTSMA**, lead pastor of Antioch Church and author of *Pursuing Justice, The Grand Paradox,* and *Create vs. Copy*

Mark Sayers has done it again with this trenchant expose of the compromised and selfish church that has become so prevalent in our day. At the same time, he manages to paint a compelling vision of a faithful community for our time.

—**ALAN HIRSCH**, author, theologian, missiologist, activist: www.alanhirsch.org

In a time when religion is in decline, few voices are more essential than that of Mark Sayers. For pastors like me trying to navigate a secularizing landscape, and for all Christians looking for ways to leave the world better than they found it, *Disappearing Church* is a must-read.

—**SCOTT SAULS**, senior pastor of Christ Presbyterian Church in Nashville, Tennessee, author of *Jesus Outside the Lines: A Way Forward for Those Who Are Tired of Taking Sides*

In *Disappearing Church*, Sayers pairs a powerful cultural analysis with pastoral wisdom on what it means to be faithful in this moment. *Disappearing Church* is a gift to the church, and will provide great encouragement to those seeking to follow Jesus in their daily lives.

—**MICHAEL WEAR**, former White House staffer and founder of Public Square Strategies LLC

From Cultural Relevance

to Gospel Resilience

MARK SAYERS

MOODY PUBLISHERS

CHICAGO

All Scripture quotations, unless otherwise indicated, are taken from the Holman Christian Standard Bible®, Copyright © 1999, 2000, 2002, 2003 by Holman Bible Publishers. Used by permission. Holman Christian Standard Bible®, Holman CSB®, and HCSB® are federally registered trademarks of Holman Bible Publishers.

Scripture quotations marked (NIV) are taken from the Holy Bible, New International Version®, NIV®. Copyright © 1973, 1978, 1984, 2011 by Biblica, Inc.™ Used by permission of Zondervan. All rights reserved worldwide. www.zondervan.com. The "NIV" and "New International Version" are trademarks registered in the United States Patent and Trademark Office by Biblica, Inc.™.

Scripture quotations marked ESV are taken from The Holy Bible, English Standard Version. Copyright © 2000, 2001 by Crossway Bibles, a division of Good News Publishers. Used by permission. All rights reserved.

Edited by Elizabeth Cody Newenhuyse
Cover design: Simplicated Studio
Interior design: Smartt Guys design

Library of Congress Cataloging-in-Publication Data
Names: Sayers, Mark.
Title: Disappearing church : from cultural relevance to gospel resilience /
  Mark Sayers.
Description: Chicago : Moody Publishers, 2016. | Includes bibliographical
  references.
Identifiers: LCCN 2015039865 | ISBN 9780802413352
Subjects: LCSH: Christianity—Forecasting. | Church.
Classification: LCC BR481 .S29 2016 | DDC 270.8/3—dc23 LC
record available at http://lccn.loc.gov/2015039865

We hope you enjoy this book from Moody Publishers. Our goal is to provide high-quality, thought-provoking books and products that connect truth to your real needs and challenges. For more information on other books and products written and produced from a biblical perspective, go to www.moodypublishers.com or write to:

Moody Publishers
820 N. La Salle Boulevard
Chicago, IL 60610

3 5 7 9 10 8 6 4

Printed in the United States of America

CONTENTS

Dark Clouds—or Glorious Sun?

Something has changed. Can you feel it?

The air temperature has suddenly dropped and strong breeze has descended. The long-watched, leaden clouds of secularism are now forebodingly overhead. Heavy drops splatter around us, promising a downpour of disbelief. Anxiously we look for shelter, for cover, for higher ground.

We wonder if the structures and shelters that surround us will withstand the impending flood. After the deluge what will stand? Which of our structures have strong enough foundations? Which trees have deep enough roots? Who has the resilience to hold on when the waters come? Before an impending storm a gnawing sense of fragility is felt in your bones. What will remain? What will disappear?

In the West we are witnessing a number of disappearances.

The ongoing disappearance of the Judeo-Christian worldview from Western culture.

The disappearance of a large segment of believers, who across the Western world are leaving churches, walking away from active faith, or faith altogether during their young adult years.

The disappearances of thousands of churches across the West, as churches close or begin the process of winding down, and as the heavily represented builder and boomer generations within the church enter their twilight years and pass from this life.

The disappearance of a mode of church engagement characterized by commitment, resilience, and sacrifice among many Western believers. In its place a new mode of disengaged Christian faith and church interaction is emerging. This new mode is characterized by sporadic engagement, passivity, commitment phobia, and a consumerist framework.

> LIVING WITH GOSPEL RESILIENCE IN THE CORROSIVE SOIL OF WESTERN CULTURE REQUIRES A POSTURE OF LIVING AS A CREATIVE MINORITY.

We had hoped that the dark clouds of secularism, promising their downpour of meaninglessness, would eventually drive Westerners into the shelter of the church. Yet as we will discover, what we view as dark clouds are viewed by many as the breaking through of a glorious sun and the arrival of warm, blue post-Christian skies.

MOVING BEYOND THE SHACKLES OF RELIGION

The post-Christian skies appear warm to an influential and increasing segment of Western culture because of an ideology. This ideology is as deeply held as any core doctrine cherished by the religiously faithful. This ideology views biblical faith through a narrow and simplistic lens, in which Christianity exists as a powerful cultural straitjacket, restraining Western culture from freedom, pleasure, and progress.

This belief, which first emerged during the Enlightenment era of the eighteenth century, holds that Western culture will flourish once orthodox religion is jettisoned, that the relegation of Christianity to history's garbage dump will result in a kind of utopia breaking out in our culture. This Enlightenment belief in the inherent baseness of religion and the unquestioned goodness of irreligion is staggeringly resilient. It has persisted despite world wars, totalitarian regimes, economic collapses, environmental crises, humanitarian disasters, and enduring poverty.

This belief also endures despite the actual realities of Christianity as it is lived in the daily lives of believers. Bemused by the intolerance of many in the West toward Christianity as it is practiced on the ground, the British politician Michael Gove writes, "The reality of Christian mission in today's churches is a story of thousands of quiet kindnesses. In many of our most disadvantaged communities it is the churches that provide warmth, food, friendship, and support for individuals who have fallen on the worst of times."[1]

Reading Gove's words I think of the former drug addict I spoke to in the street last week who upon becoming a Christian kicked her habit and now spends her spare time visiting addicts in low-income housing. I think of the Catholic thrift shop I just bought a second-hand book from this morning—a wonderfully ramshackle affair, staffed by smiling, elderly volunteers and new immigrants, giving their time to help the poor. Both examples illustrate Gove's reminder that "the lives of most clergy and the thoughts of most churchgoers are not occupied with agonizing over sexual morality but with helping others in practical ways—in proving their commitment to Christ in service to others."

Yet despite this gloriously redemptive and charmingly mundane reality of the kingdom of God at play, the persistent belief still holds sway that the West must move beyond the perceived oppressive shackles of religion.

THE SOFT POWER OF POST-CHRISTIANITY

I lean back in my chair as my coffee sits in front of me, adorned with latte art, a now internationally recognized symbol, operating as a kind of universally approved stamp of quality. The specials, written on a chalkboard, herald an inventive mashup of international dishes and guilt-nullifying organic ingredients. All around me the café is designed to within an inch of its life, including the regulation hints of Scandinavian modernism, accent of raw industrialism, plus a few playful nods to '80s street art.

On the wall a cork board is filled with all kinds of posters offering countless opportunities for fun and self-improvement. Posters that implore you to experience an intimate, acoustic gig in a vineyard. Others to lose yourself in the sweaty hedonism of an international deep house DJ's set. Invitations to improve your mind and your body with Bikram Yoga, to join the fight against climate change. So many options, so many possibilities, so many choices. Yet the promises of the posters speak out in vain, ignored by the customers who sit and stand bewitched by the thin screens in their hands, screens offering even more options, options as vast as the Internet itself.

Spreading across the Western world like a slow-growing moss, this beautiful culture seemed to offer us everything. More money, more stuff, more options; but then the global financial crisis pulled the excess back, and a new kind of beautiful culture took hold. This was more handcrafted, more artisanal, more organic, more designed, more curated, and definitely more expensive. It's easy to be appalled by conspicuous consumption, but this was a different, more alluring beast. It's hard to resist such an onslaught of delicate beauty.

Not that there's anything wrong with what I observed in the café. Rather, combined, the options of post-Christianity operate in the mode of what foreign affairs experts call "soft power," an indirect yet powerful sort of influence. They don't bludgeon you out of your faith;

they subtly coax you, each option quietly proclaiming a kind of gospel in itself, in which the good life can be yours.

This soft power is lubricated by technology and the promise of consumerism. Through the mythologies of advertising, media, the Internet, and the instructive example of celebrity, a vast mental world is daily constructed in our minds, painting the possibility of a godless utopia—a secular heaven on earth in which an individual life infused with pleasure, peace, and possibility is achievable this side of death.

Therefore, the final checkmate of this secularist coup is accomplished not by a frontal assault upon theology, but by a practical atheism that offers the fruit of shalom minus the tree of biblical faith that bore it. What is most striking about this secularist creed is its persistence in the face of the reality of human life. We all suffer, we yearn, we age, we sicken, we die. Yet Western culture clings tightly to its faith in the arrival of the godless utopia and the possibility of a human life untainted by suffering.

THE GOSPEL OF SELF

What we are experiencing is not the eradication of God from the Western mind, but rather the enthroning of the self as the greatest authority. God is increasingly relegated to the role of servant, and massager of the personal will. We will find that progressive, contemporary Western culture is shaped by an ancient heresy—Gnosticism. Gnosticism at its heart is an alternate gospel, which moves authority from God to the self, in which the individual seeks to power their own development and salvation.

Gnosticism views God as distant and flawed; therefore it seeks to move beyond God. This Gnostic influence shapes a desire to create a post-Christian culture. A deepening cultural mood seeks to move beyond orthodox Christianity, to refashion its beliefs and practices to fit the spirit of the day. The battle lines in the clash are found in issues relating to the individual will. This mood is also felt within the church. Scot McKnight observes that contemporary Christianity "has increasingly displaced the Bible as its foundation for knowing what to think and how to live and supplanted it with experience, desire, and preference. In other words, it has surrendered its heart to personal freedoms."[2] Our challenge, therefore, is not found just outside the walls of the church—it is also within.

This book will argue that we cannot solely rely on the contemporary, Western church's favored strategy of cultural relevance, in which Christianity and the church is made "relevant" to secular Western culture. Instead we need to rediscover gospel resilience. To walk the countercultural narrow path in which we die to self and re-throne God in our lives as the supreme authority. In our culture of radical individualism, with its Gnostic hue, no other approach will suffice.

Living with gospel resilience in the corrosive soil of Western culture requires a posture of living as a creative minority. Throughout history God has replenished cultures, through the witness of minorities of believers who hold true to their beliefs while blessing the surrounding culture. It is to this position we must return. However, to live with gospel resilience as a creative minority, we must come to grips with the essential nature of our post-Christian age. To this we will turn our attention next.

Gospel resilience

PART I

UNDERSTANDING OUR CRAVING FOR CULTURAL RELEVANCE

Chapter I

Our Current Post-Christianity

"It's the usual utopian vision. . . . I mean, like everything else you guys are pushing, it sounds perfect, sounds progressive, but it carries with it more control. . . . And that's what's so scary. Individually you don't know what you are doing collectively."

Dave Eggers, *The Circle*

MOVING PAST GOD

Within the church in the West it is almost universally acknowledged that we live in a post-Christian culture. However, it is crucial that we understand what we mean by post-Christian. Many have understood post-Christianity as a kind of religious year zero, a mass amnesia in which the West has forgotten its Christian past, and in which we have returned to a kind of pre-Christian reality. As we will discover in chapter 3, this assumption can have dramatic effects on how we perceive the task of mission in the West. Post-Christianity is not pre-Christianity; rather post-Christianity attempts to move beyond Christianity, whilst simultaneously feasting upon its fruit.

Post-Christian culture attempts to retain the solace of faith, whilst gutting it of the costs, commitments, and restraints that the gospel places upon the individual will. Post-Christianity intuitively yearns for the justice and shalom of the kingdom, whilst defending the reign of the individual will. Post-Christianity is Christianity emptied of its content, as theologian Henri de Lubac would warn:

> *Forms of atheistic humanism often preserved a number of values that were Christian in origin; but having cut off these values from their source, they were powerless to maintain them in their full strength or even in their authentic integrity. Spirit, reason, liberty, truth, brotherhood, justice: these great things, without which there is no true humanity . . . quickly become unreal when no longer seen as a radiation from God, when faith in the living God no longer provides their vital substance. Then they become empty forms.*[1]

Yet despite such warnings, post-Christianity grows. *New York Times* columnist David Brooks senses this post-Christian, individualist theology in the wisdom and advice given to university students: "They are sent off into this world with the . . . theology ringing in their ears. If you sample some of the commencement addresses being broadcast on C-Span these days, you see that many graduates are told to: Follow your passion, chart your own course, march to the beat of your own drummer, follow your dreams and find yourself. This is the litany of expressive individualism."[2] Sadly such advice can be found not only in the secular college commencement speech, but also in many churches, albeit with the saccharine sheen of a Christianized veneer, as the post-Christian mood affects even Christianity itself.

THE NEW POWERS

To get to the heart of our post-Christian context we must understand how we got here, how the ground shifted. Sometime in the night a revolution occurred and we did not notice it. So distracted by the phony war between left and right, conservatives and liberals, we have failed to notice that a new power had seized control of both our imaginations and the halls of power. This new power swirls around a small yet widely held set of beliefs:

1. The highest good is individual freedom, happiness, self-definition, and self-expression.

2. Traditions, religions, received wisdom, regulations, and social ties that restrict individual freedom, happiness, self-definition, and self-expression must be reshaped, deconstructed, or destroyed.

3. The world will inevitably improve as the scope of individual freedom grows. Technology—in particular the Internet—will motor this progression toward utopia.

4. The primary social ethic is tolerance of everyone's self-defined quest for individual freedom and self-expression. Any deviation from this ethic of tolerance is dangerous and must not be tolerated. Therefore social justice is less about economic or class inequality, and more about issues of equality relating to individual identity, self-expression, and personal autonomy.

5. Humans are inherently good.

6. Large-scale structures and institutions are suspicious at best and evil at worst.

7. Forms of external authority are rejected and personal authenticity is lauded.

Political historian Mark Lilla notes that the simplicity of these beliefs means that they are held by seemingly opposed groups in the West. These beliefs are held dear by groups as disparate as human rights advocates, pornography producers, free-market economists, leftist anarchists, Internet hackers, gay marriage campaigners, hippies, tech entrepreneurs, and small-government conservatives. Behind much of the rhetoric these views hold sway for much of the left and right. However, most importantly for millions across the West, these beliefs provide the dominant framework for navigating life.

This new cultural outlook is not so much an ideology but something that borders on a religious belief, which for Lilla "sanctions ignorance about the world, and therefore blinds adherents to its effects in that world. It begins with basic liberal principles—the sanctity of the individual, the priority of freedom, distrust of public authority, tolerance—and advances no further. It has no taste for reality, no curiosity about how we got here or where we are going. . . . It has no interest in institutions and has nothing to say about the necessary, and productive, tension between individual and collective purposes." What makes this contemporary outlook almost religious is its unquestioned faith that all we need to do "is give individuals maximum freedom in every aspect of their lives and all will be well."[3]

> SOMETIME IN THE NIGHT A REVOLUTION OCCURRED AND WE DID NOT NOTICE IT.

These beliefs have not so much been argued as assumed. They are not enforced; rather they are imbibed. We do not receive them as intellectual propaganda to be obeyed. Instead they are communicated to us at an almost subconscious level through the high priests of advertising and the techno prophets of Silicon Valley. This new cultural mood becomes all the more powerful as the good is reduced to mere individual happiness. We can no longer see beyond ourselves, to learn from history or be concerned about the future. "The result is an amnesia about everything except the immediate, the instant, the now, and the me,"[4] worries media theorist Andrew Keen. The future is not left to God, but rather a kind of implicit, fuzzy faith that things will simply move to get better. Somehow society will get better. My life will get better.

This faith in progress both societal and personal, which requires little of the individual, whilst promising maximum happiness, is an attractive proposition to many, both outside of the church and within. The journalist Malcolm Muggeridge, having found faith at the end of his life, observed and anticipated the post-Christian mood taking hold: "The whole social structure is now tumbling down, dethroning its God, undermining its certainties. And all this, wonderfully enough, in the name of the health, wealth and happiness of all mankind. In the moral vacuum left by this emptying Christianity of its spiritual or transcendental content . . . is its opposite—life enhancement."[5] As we will learn, this emptying of faith of its content and desire for life enhancement is one of the great engines driving the disappearing church. It also is one of the great engines driving a new form of hopeful secularism. A kind of Western disbelief with a religious tone.

THEY LIKE JESUS BUT NOT CHURCH . . . OR DO THEY?

The Sunday Assembly is a hip, contemporary congregation in the heart of central London. It is filled with progressive, passionate, and idealistic attendees. The congregation sings along to contemporary music. There are messages given, social gatherings, offerings, kids clubs, midweek small groups, and social justice projects for the community. The Sunday Assembly, however, is not your typical church. It is a church for atheists.

The Sunday Assembly started as an idea of two Londoners who wanted to enjoy church without belief. The Sunday Assembly distances itself from militant atheists, instead preferring a friendly, accepting culture. While the movement is theology-free, it intuitively gathers around the values of tolerance, progressive values, and personal development. The London congregation quickly outgrew their three-hundred-seat space. Since 2013, 480 congregations have been planted out of London in key cities across the Western world. The movement has struck a chord with many millennial attendees. Its global conference, called Wonder, features leadership workshops, advice on planting from a former-pastor-and-planter-turned-atheist, and help on growing healthy congregations from the son of a prominent Christian author and speaker, who has moved from being a "progressive Christian" to a humanist atheist.

Spearheading the rationale behind this new kind of atheistic gathering is philosopher and bestselling author Alain de Botton's book *Religion for Atheists*. De Botton argues, like many of the attendees of the atheist church, that contemporary culture is an alienating place. Not that church was alienating, but contemporary culture was alienating. While these congregants disagreed with faith, they felt that contemporary culture lacked the communal and institutional benefits that churches and communities of faith brought. One of the great mantras of church strategy in the West has been that people liked Jesus, but they did not like church. This was a mantra for many who were seeking to make Christianity relevant. Now, this new atheist church movement has turned this maxim on its head. These people did not like Jesus, but they liked church.

While the original congregation in London has stayed strong, its plants across the globe are smaller. Time will tell whether the growth of the atheist church movement has traction. In the nineteenth century the atheist philosopher August Comte launched a movement of unbelieving congregations; however, most of his congregations struggled to last beyond a single generation. The Sunday Assembly faces the same challenge faced by religious communities of disengaged, radical individualism. However, the appearance of the Sunday Assembly points toward the essence of our post-Christian culture—that is, the desire to retain elements of Christianity while still moving past it.

A HISTORY OF POST-CHRISTIANITY

The idea that Western culture needs to move beyond orthodox Christianity into a post-Christian age can be traced back as far as the thought of the medieval theologian Joachim of Fiore. Joachim hoped for a future epoch of the Holy Spirit, in which the gospel of Christ would be transcended by a new order of love, and the church replaced by a new, spiritualized elite. Hope would not be in the return of Christ but in the arrival of an enlightened future, an idea that is central to post-Christianity. Moving beyond the age of Christ defined by the enfleshed, incarnational contours of the church, the epoch of the Spirit would be the age of the spiritually autonomous individual who has moved beyond mediating institutions, concrete expression, and the sacraments of the church. This is the essence of the idea of post-Christianity: the idea of a purer, less concrete form of Christianity emerging out of Christianity itself.

The political philosopher Eric Voegelin comments on this innovation: "We can recognize, even in this thoroughly Christian context, the first symptoms of the idea of a post-Christian era."[6] We can see also the germ in Joachim's three-part division of history that would grow into the trisecting of history into ancient-medieval-modern. This is the foundation of the belief that Western, developed culture is more progressive, enlightened, and evolved than other cultures. Hope then lies not in God, but in being on the right side of history.

A LIBERAL CHRISTIAN CULTURE

We can see in the trajectory of thought that grows out of Joachim's age of the Spirit the genesis of the notion that the church must emerge and evolve into a higher, purer, and progressed form. The

German philosopher Schelling, building upon Joachim's age of the Spirit, predicted a coming age of perfected Christianity, creating the idea of a liberal or progressive Christianity. The thought that Christianity must change and evolve into a new progressive form is ubiquitous both inside and outside of the church. Anytime anyone complains that the church must evolve its core theology with the times to stay relevant, or that the church's future is found in ditching the structures, institutions, and forms of "organized religion" and embrace a fuzzy notion of "community" or "spirituality," we can detect Joachim's fingerprints.

Reflecting on our current religious and cultural landscape, the cultural critic Joseph Bottum further sharpens our understanding of post-Christianity. For Bottum, our cultural post-Christianity bears a tremendous likeness to liberal Christianity, in particular its Protestant forms. Liberal Christianity grew alongside modernity, attempting to reshape faith and theology around the worldview of the Enlightenment. Miracles, the supernatural, and Scripture were viewed through the lens of skeptical scientism. A more materialist faith was formed, which removed the transcendent elements of Christianity and focused the believer's attention on an achievable kingdom of God that could be shaped by responsible and diligent human hands.

From the end of the nineteenth century to the middle of the twentieth, liberal Christianity won over the leadership of a great part of the Western mainline denominations. These leaders saw liberal Christianity as the correct response to the rise of modernity. However, as countercultural and transcendent elements of faith were removed, liberal churches began to bleed believers. The exact opposite occurred to what many had predicted: the churches that retained countercultural and transcendent elements and maintained orthodox theologies grew, while those who had abandoned central elements of Christian theology declined at spectacular rates.

Over a few decades, once-strong denominations became a pale shadow of their former strength. In the exodus out of these churches, Bottum notes that many made their way into growing evangelical churches and others joined the Catholic Church. Crucially, many simply stopped going to church, and in the process migrated their liberal Christianity into the wider culture. Like a team of suicide bombers who obliterate themselves yet irrevocably change the cultural atmosphere, liberal Christianity has essentially destroyed itself as an ecclesiological, institutional force, yet has won the culture over to its vision of a Christianity reshaped for contemporary tastes.

While cursory glances at our culture's religious hue can give one the impression of atheism, we will soon see its liberal Christian residue. Following liberal Christianity's lead, the majority of Westerners hold to a belief in a pleasant afterlife and a benevolent Christian-esque God. However, the doctrines of divine judgment and hell are ditched as repugnantly retrograde. Concepts of personal morality and the pursuit of virtue are replaced by a desire for the communal good. The dogma of the kingdom of God and the coming New Jerusalem exists, but is reframed as the pursuit and possibility of a perfected, inclusive, civil society. Satan and the possibility of personal evil and sin remerges in a new depersonalized form, as Bottum explains: "Sin, in other words, appears as a social fact and the redeemed personality becomes confident about its own salvation by being aware of that fact. By knowing about, and rejecting, the evil that darkens society."[7]

MANY OF THOSE WHO LEAVE THE CHURCH DON'T IMAGINE THAT THEY ARE THROWING THEMSELVES INTO AN ATHEISTIC SEA.

In this reformulated understanding of sin and evil, salvation is achieved through the gaining of enlightened attitude. For the privileged post-Christian, this realization comes as a kind of revelation that can be used as a badge of power. Thus those who have gained this enlightened attitude, who see the world for what it is, form a re-fashioned concept of the biblical notion of the elect. This community of the elect has moved beyond the need for concrete forms of church and association, and instead form a culture based on shared opinion manifested in a language based on a correctness of speech, opinion, and belief.

LEAVING CHURCH

Once we grasp that our post-Christian world is shaped by a lib-eral Christianity, we can understand better the phenomenon of church-leavers, especially amongst young adults. There have always been those who have left the church over doubts, just as there have al-ways been those who left to pursue pleasure without account. When we understand that post-Christian culture offers a kind of alternative, liberal form of Christianity, we can see that many of those who leave don't imagine that they are throwing themselves into an atheistic sea. Instead, they are retaining their faith, albeit in a reframed form. Half a century ago such people would have probably moved from conser-vative churches to more liberal mainline ones. Now with the culture reflecting the values of the liberal mainline churches, one simply leaves the church.

If the transcendent elements of faith are ignored or softened, if sin is recast as purely unenlightened attitudes, if evil is viewed as "out there," existent in only structural forms, if the hope of the kingdom is re-imagined as achievable through activism and sound policy, if a culture exists within the church of Christian self-hatred, it is only a matter of time before one discovers that there are moral, happy peo-ple outside the church, who are spiritual and who wish for a culture of fairness and inclusion too. One day the penny drops, and one won-ders if they can still have what they value about their faith without the restrictions and prohibitions of creedal, communal Christianity. The cultural mood shudders toward the drive to become good. The individual, in his own power, perhaps with the aid of the cultural tide of progression, must become good.

THE DESIRE TO BE GOOD

J. K. A. Smith detects in this new moral order a return to another ancient Christian heresy, Pelagianism,[8] the belief that salvation can be attained and that human perfectibility is reachable through pure human effort. Pelagianism takes its name from Pelagius, a fifth-century British-Roman Christian theologian who held to the belief that humans could reach perfection through their own efforts. Pelagius taught that evil was a result of humans making bad choices. These choices, and by extension evil, could be removed through the making of good choices, gaining education, and practicing self-control. This was an attractive view to many, and around Pelagius coalesced a group of young believers from the elite strata of Roman society. Historian Peter Brown writes:

> Pelagianism had appealed to a universal theme: the need of the individual to define himself, and to feel free to create his own values in the midst of the conventional, second-rate life of society. . . . The families, whose members Pelagius addressed, had lapsed gradually into Christianity by mixed marriages and political conformity. This meant that the conventional "good man" of pagan Rome had quite unthinkingly become the conventional "good Christian" of the fifth century.[9]

Attractive to this young Christian elite was the idea that if sin could be removed through individual effort, the real locus of evil was found in the surrounding pagan society. A surrounding pagan society then could be reformed through the example of a church of virtuous and heroic Christian individuals. Jesus' injunction to practice good

IN THE POST-CHRISTIAN IMAGINATION, TO HOLD THE WRONG MORAL OPINIONS WILL NOT SEND ONE TO HELL, BUT IT COULD SEE YOU SENT TO THE OUTER SOCIAL DARKNESS, TO GNASH YOUR TEETH IN SOCIAL IRRELEVANCE.

deeds in secrecy was forgotten as the Pelagians then became grand "virtue signalers," broadcasting their dramatic renunciations of wealth and privilege and their programs of social improvement in an attempt to impress the public into faith.

Pelagianism appealed to those who were accustomed to power, control, and privilege, and who found the doctrine of original sin insulting. At its core, Pelagianism had a Gnostic belief in the individual's potential to control his own salvation. The idea that Adam's sin had corrupted the whole of humanity was rejected by the Pelagians as too binding and restrictive. For Pelagians, the rejection of original sin meant the accepting of the damnation of those who are not able to achieve human perfection.

HELL AS SOCIAL ISOLATION AND SHAMING

For if human perfection is easily achieved through sensible choices and a decorous self-control, the human who fails, sins, lusts, and envies is justifiably damnable. In the Pelagianism of our contemporary post-Christianity—in which perfection and morality can be achieved by adopting the progressive cultural sensibilities—we fear a different kind of damnation. In the post-Christian imagination, to hold the wrong moral opinions will not send one to hell, but it could see you sent to the outer social darkness, to gnash your teeth in social irrelevance.

The North African bishop Augustine was God's man to answer Pelagius's heresy. In contrast to Pelagius's simplified understanding of sin and evil, Augustine saw in Scripture a much more nuanced truth concerning human imperfection. Beneath our sensible decisions to do right lay a much more complicated subterranean and subconscious sea of discordant desires. The public "virtue signaling" of the Pelagians could seem noble on the surface, but could also disguise a prideful attempt to gain public affirmation. Augustine saw humans trapped in a permanent state of dislocation. This dislocation was driven by the rupturing of their relationship with God, a rupturing caused by human rebellion and pride. If Pelagius was right about sin, then we can all under our own steam adjust our own behavior and achieve perfection. However, if Augustine is correct, that our desires are disordered, running amok, and seeking God in all the wrong places, then only reconciliation with God can save us. For as the Gospels tell us, only Christ can truly see into the heart of man. Salvation does not come as a work of self-improvement, but as a divine shock, an undeserved gift given.

The Pelagian or post-Christian practitioner working toward their own moral self-improvement by seeking salvation by their own hand ultimately can only offer up praise to themselves. By bidding farewell to divinely revealed notions of morality and righteousness, we welcome into our lives the constant worry over our own goodness. The Pharisees parade their piety to be affirmed in their goodness. The post-Christian revolution, by removing God from the throne in preference of the self, cannot look to a transcendent Almighty for a definition of righteousness, morality, and justice. The self must determine what the good is.

The post-Christian robbed of God as a moral standard must "virtue signal" instead to prove their goodness to others, surrounding themselves with others who will mirror back and affirm their goodness, while casting pharisaical accusations and curses of outrage down upon those who do not hold the correct moral line. In reframing Christianity, the post-Christian births a reframed puritanical approach to morality. While our post-Christian age has divested itself of attaching any morality to sexuality (barring rape and the abuse of minors), it approaches health, food, and the body with a puritanical fervor.

THE BEAUTIFUL WORLD IS WALLED

I am looking at a photo taken where Augustine lived and wrote in the northernmost part of Africa. In the foreground, two women in brightly colored polo shirts and immaculate white pants play golf on an even more immaculate green course. They are self-creating, sophisticated citizens of the beautiful world enjoying life. In the background there is an incredibly high cyclone fence, and perched precariously atop it are at least fifty people, their dark, dirty clothes a complete contrast to the women in the foreground. Behind the fence is not a lush golfing green but dirt. The cyclone fence is the border between Morocco and the tiny part of Spanish territory in North Africa, a legacy of colonialism. The men atop the fence are African refugees waiting for the right moment to climb down into the European Union and attempt to find their place in the beautiful world.

> THE "INCLUSIVE" WEST AT ITS CORE IS BUILT UPON EXCLUSION.

The progressive, tolerant, beautiful post-Christian world is increasingly becoming a walled city. Inside the beautiful world, a growing clamor for inclusion attempts to allow its citizens absolute freedom, yet at the same time the borders are secured, keeping the masses of poor and displaced people out. The West congratulates itself on its tolerance and exclusivity; however, our passports, citizenship papers, and armed border guards illustrate the true ethic of inclusion and equality held by the West. The "inclusive" West at its core is built upon exclusion. At its heart it reaches for the kingdom, but falls short.

POST-CHRISTIANITY IS A GRACELESS FAITH

Just as the Pelagians saw themselves as a moral force, advocating and beckoning the church toward moral improvement, so today the post-Christian culture looks down upon the church, beckoning it to lose its "immorality" and evolve toward virtue. However, the moral evolution they beckon the church toward is a religion minus grace. Without an understanding of the primal originality of human sin, post-Christianity is blind to its own control, its own power, its own weaknesses. The rejection of original sin divides us because evil is seen as "out there." The post-Christian society, which denies its own Christian underpinnings, falls into the trap of religiosity. Because it is religious and yet denies its own sinfulness, it must blame the other. The right blames the "illegal immigrant," the left the "uneducated working class" or "unsophisticated rural folk."

THE FREEDOM IN DISCOVERING OUR OWN FALLENNESS

We now as a culture prefer the authentic, the organic, the homemade and homegrown, the approachable, the touchable, the human, and the natural. These things seem to offer us an ethos of goodness minus the boundaries and parameters of traditional definitions of sin. Yet they are impotent in the face of raw evil. The contemporary liberal ethos of not doing something that harms another believes—influenced by materialistic underpinnings—that harm is only physical. To be good news to a world that does not know or acknowledge the full weight of evil and thus cannot treat it, we must again rediscover the full weight and eternal nature of wrongdoing.

The visual representations that amounted to virtue and morality in the Roman world could not be true indicators of rightness with God, for only Christ could truly see into the hearts of humans. Programs of moral self-improvement minus God naturally veer either to love at the expense of justice or justice at the expense of love.

The Pelagians of Augustine's time demanded justice of those who do not love according to their standards, while demanding that they be loved and being blind to the ways in which they deserved to be held to divine justice.

The post-Christian revolution is a kind of Christian revolution minus Christ, in which the enemy is always the other, in which justice is always sought externally. The Christian revolution demanded the death of the king, but not the king that sat in a palace; rather it demanded the death of the kings and queens who ate of the fruit in the garden. However, at the height of the revolution the only good King, the only monarch who ruled with justice and righteousness, who did not deserve to be toppled, allowed Himself to be executed, so that we with all our pretenses of royalty would not have to die for our unjust rule.

The cross held both love and justice together. The gift of grace caused humans to fall at the foot of the cross, understanding that they were sinful, only then to be picked up into the loving arms of Christ to find that they were children of God. The exclusivity of the cross was the doorway to the inclusivity of the kingdom. A kingdom that will not come in fullness through the self-effort of enlightened hands and opinions, but when Christ Himself returns with justice and love. Then we will discover a vision of justice far broader than our narrow contemporary conceptions, one that has answers not just for those inside the cyclone fencing of the beautiful world.

Chapter 2

The History of "Relevant"

THE SEARCH FOR RELEVANCE

The period during and immediately following World War Two was a high point for the church in the Western world. Despite the ongoing hostility of cultural elites, churchgoing attendance was significant in the United States, Britain, and even my own country of Australia. The horror of war and the specter of political movements such as Nazism and Communism had seen a whole host of intellectuals and writers such as T. S. Eliot, W. H. Auden, Evelyn Waugh, and Graham Greene embrace or return to Christian faith. C. S. Lewis's wartime BBC lectures on Christianity had gripped the United Kingdom. Evangelicalism was emerging from its cultural seclusion into an evangelistic force, notably through the ministry of a new cadre of popular preachers, most famously Billy Graham. To be sure, the period was in no way a truly idyllic epoch of Christian influence: underneath the surface, various forces, thinkers, and movements all corrosive to Christian faith bubbled away, soon to erupt like geysers. However, this period is worth outlining as a comparison to our current time, as an era when

Christianity carved out a small but respectable place within the public square.

As the 1960s progressed, things began to change. A cultural revolution broke out, a revolution that contained contradictory streams. The stream that sought a more communitarian approach to life and a desire for culture-wide justice struck a chord with prophetic elements within the church, from civil rights campaigner Martin Luther King Jr. to the widely read activist Catholic monk Thomas Merton. However, the spirit of the '60s paradoxically also contained desire for a radical personal autonomy, a shedding of inherited cultural wisdom and prohibitions, and questioning of not just corrupt authority, but of all authority.

FROM POLITICS TO PSYCHOLOGY

This rebellion against all inherited authority led to the enshrinement of the individual as the highest authority. By the 1970s, the communal spirit and desire for culture-wide change had been subverted into a quest into the self. The novelist Tom Wolfe famously labeled the 1970s The Me Decade. The desire for societal change devolved into a pursuit of self-development. This was evidenced as the famed 1960s countercultural radical Abbie Hoffman by the 1970s proclaimed that "it is more important to get [your] own head together than to move multitudes."[1] Hoffman's partner in cultural revolution, Jerry Rubin, retreated from the political struggle to embrace an endless array of New Age practices and therapies. The new belief was that truth was not to be found in class struggle or political consciousness, but rather in the journey into the self. Politics had been superseded by psychology. The countercultural revolution had morphed into a therapeutic quest to discover individual fulfillment.

RAISING OUR EXPECTATIONS OF LIFE

This new journey into the self saw a fundamental shift occur in what the average person expected out of life. Our desire for personal freedom and autonomy expanded rapidly. The church again struggled to keep up with this change. However, as it is prone to do, it adapted. By the end of the '70s, the evangelical movement that had begun to engage with the culture in the wake of the war had moved into a position of prominence. Evangelicalism had always placed a high emphasis on personal faith and a tangible communion with God in the innermost parts of life. Thus by the conclusion of the decade, evangelicalism's emphasis resonated, as many found their inner journey leading them back into the church.

THE RISE OF THE CONTEMPORARY CHURCH

The beginning of the '80s saw the rise of the contemporary church movement. Missionaries returning home from the Two-Thirds World found their home culture secularizing, and they began to adapt some of the missiological methods that they had learned on the mission field back home in the West. They began to look to the corporate world to gain insights that might aid the church. This train of thought grew into the church growth movement. A growing belief that secularism could be arrested by an emphasis on relevance began to take hold. Our best chance at growth seemed to lie in culturally relevant forms of church, expression, and communication.

Many of the pioneers of the church growth movement were members of the first great youth generation—the baby boomers. Moving into positions of organizational influence, the boomers brought their own generational style with them, in particular a focus on youthfulness and casualness. Many had come to faith or been influenced by the Jesus People, a radical Christian movement that had flowered within the countercultural hippie movement of the '60s. The '60s had seen a generation gap emerge between the younger boomers with their desire for progress and social change and their "builder" parents who yearned for stability after the chaos of the World Wars and the Depression. The boomers brought this generational tension into the conversation regarding the future shape of the church. It was here that the primary battle lines were drawn between traditional and contemporary models of church, stirring up the question of how far the church should pursue relevance.

DESPITE THE SUCCESS OF MANY CONTEMPORARY CHURCHES, THE SECULARIZING JUGGERNAUT THUNDERED ON AROUND THEM.

As the church growth movement grew, denominational distinctives began to recede. Believers chose churches according to their tastes rather than their denominational heritage. Previous emphases on dogma, doctrine, and ecclesiastical authority were replaced by a taste for community, experience, and the relational. The assumed belief was that people were uninterested in Christianity because they found church traditions and rituals alien and unwelcoming. If the church could be made relevant—with culturally relevant forms instead of traditions and ritualized trappings—then Christianity would flourish in the Western world again. Flourish is what many contemporary churches did, as traditional and mainline churches began to decline. Yet despite the success of many contemporary churches, the secularizing juggernaut thundered on around them.

THE BLOWBACK

The contemporary church model thrived in American soil. Americans' staggeringly high appetite for church attendance, standardization, and franchising, accompanied by a significant reservoir of latent Christians who were only an invite away from re-engaging with the church, ensured that the model, if done right, could succeed. However, in other parts of the West, namely the United Kingdom, Australia, New Zealand, and Western Europe, the model struggled to work as they found themselves further down the road of secularization.

For a growing group of practitioners, the contemporary church movement did not seem the answer it appeared to be in the United States. Yes, there were contemporary churches in those countries that grew, but often they were in those nations' own "Bible belts" and historically Christian regions. Without large numbers of church shoppers and latent Christians, the contemporary churches were less successful. As a result, new experimental approaches began to be initiated. In Britain expressions like the Nine O'Clock Service in Sheffield,[2] an experimental Anglican service, blended elements of traditional liturgical worship with the emerging electronic dance music culture. The Nine O'Clock Service seemed to indicate a kind of future beyond the contemporary church, attracting thousands of attendees.

> POSTMODERNISM BECAME THE ULTIMATE JUSTIFICATION FOR ANY KIND OF CHANGE ONE WANTED TO EFFECT WITHIN THE CHURCH.

Numerous worship experiments were spawned, under the awkward labels of "alternative worship" and "the emerging church." Many of these experiments grew alongside the Internet, eventually spreading their influence stateside, where the strong Christian media, conference, and publishing industry would grow these overseas whispers into a loud American conversation that no one could ignore.

RELEVANCE X 2

As the economic boom of the '80s began to slow into the economic downturn of the beginning of the '90s, a new mood began to take hold. Surprisingly, alternative music and culture became mainstream, and many began to look at the contemporary church with its corporate influences, middle-of-the-road rock worship, and desire for relevance as widely irrelevant. The media's fascination with the emerging Generation X—some of them the children of the baby boomers—also began to affect the conversation. For the boomers who had defined themselves by their youthfulness and rejection of their parents' values, the arrival of a new generation now defining themselves against the boomers came as a shock. A kind of panic swept the Christian cultural landscape. If this new generation was defining themselves against contemporary church, what was to be done? The need for an even more radical approach to relevance seemed only to be given more impetus by a discussion that began to grip the evangelical world around the cultural condition of postmodernism.

The theory of postmodernity, with its diagnosis that we have reached the end of the modern period, and by extension therefore the kind of culture in which the contemporary church would thrive, suited the agenda of many emerging Generation Xers. These younger leaders were advocating for a move beyond the contemporary model and a new way of engaging a secularizing culture. Postmodernism was used as a kind of stun grenade to shake up the current order that existed within evangelicalism. It became the ultimate justification for any kind of change one wanted to effect within the church.

The call for "relevance" now gained a more desperate tone, and numerous solutions were advanced. The emerging church movement, the missional church movement, the new reformed movement, the new monastic movement, and new forms of Pentecostalism, all in some way were birthed out of the idea that postmodernity was here and the church needed to respond. Even the contemporary church was changed, and the Nine O'Clock Service in Sheffield, England, with its pioneering use of music, images, and video projections—so radical at the time—is now standard fare in today's contemporary churches and conferences. Today there is a generation of millennial leaders emerging into key leadership positions within the church who have known nothing but the strategy of cultural relevance. Leaders and believers have unwittingly absorbed the belief that one can maintain both strong Christian faith and social currency within Western contemporary culture with little or no friction.

THE DISAPPEARING RELEVANT CHURCHES OF THE CONTEMPORARY WEST

Despite the contemporary church's decades-long quest for cultural relevance, it continues to struggle to gain ground in the secular West. The aging profile of the church inevitably means that many churches are demographically disappearing. Intriguingly, churches that pursued cultural relevance with the greatest gusto have also suffered their own disappearances. Those who have pursued a policy of relevance in their theology—attempting to reshape their theology into unorthodox forms to suit the contours of contemporary sensibilities—suffer the fate that liberal churches have throughout church history: inevitable decline and eventual disappearance. Other churches and movements that keep their theology orthodox but, in an attempt to be relevant to contemporary Western culture, jettison traditional church structures and forms, disappear as viable entities a handful of years later.

THE FUTURE IS A CLEAN, PROGRESSIVE, NORTHERN EUROPEAN CITY

Because postmodernity is predicated on the collapse of the structures of modernity, there was a belief and a hope that as the modern project fell—a project that had alienated the West from God—there would be a great turning back to spirituality and God as culture became more bleak. Many felt the future would look like Ridley Scott's *Blade Runner*, or a William Gibson cyberpunk novel. The bleakness and failures of Western culture would make faith attractive again.

But in the '90s the Canadian author Douglas Coupland predicted that the future would look like Bonn—the clean, well-ordered, and modern German city. He was right: the future of the West increasingly looks like a Scandinavian city or my hometown of Melbourne, voted the world's most livable city, where there are amazing coffee shops, creative industries, great public transport, and a new civil religion of tolerance and progressive values. Even the most culturally influential cities of the United States are morphing into this form. As we will discover in chapter 3, such places provide an incredible missional challenge.

FROM POSTMODERN TO METAMODERN

The Dutch cultural theorists Timotheus Vermeulen and Robin van den Akker note that our cultural mood has shifted from the postmodern mood of cynicism and irony, to what they label as metamodernism.[3] The era of postmodern irony and cynicism has been replaced by what they label as the "new sincerity," which is visible across Western culture and can be seen in the new folk music movement, the films of Wes Anderson, and the novels of Michael Chabon and Zadie Smith. Vermeulen and van den Akker use the term "meta" to prefix modern in the sense of swinging between poles, not learning from either pole, but simply bouncing between sincerity and being overwhelmed, between hope and anxiety, between modernity and postmodernity. This metamodern mood still wants to deconstruct, but not wantonly. Rather, by deconstructing beliefs, conventions, and traditions, it believes it can create a better world. It is cultural deconstruction with a messianic purpose. It believes that we can have a better world, but it is not sure how to get there.

This cultural deconstruction with a messianic purpose provides a great challenge for the church's public stance. For much of the last twenty years, a large segment of the church has taken a position of repentance of its past sins. It has become concerned about how it has appeared—exclusive, intolerant, closed-minded, and judgmental. It has worried about how it has pushed its values on other cultures—told, not listened; lectured, not conversed. Thus within Christianity in the West, a whole new posture has emerged, one that attempts to be more inclusive, more conversant, and more tolerant. Much of this has been good. Yet this move has occurred simultaneously with the culture becoming more prepared to condemn, judge, and speak in the language of right and wrong.

FLASHMOB CHURCHES

With the fall of modernity, we wishfully believed that individualism would fall as well. We believed that there was a desire and return toward community. If we could reposition around this new desire for community, then we could find a fruitful place within Western culture. There was a desire for community, yet this desire was held alongside an even greater desire for individual autonomy. The West had entered a truly post-institutional age, in which individuals adopted a social posture of disengagement. Social networking and other forms of pseudo-community filled the spaces where embodied community and institutions once existed. Despite the desire of many to again engage in institutional, communal life—such as the people drawn to the Sunday Assembly—many know nothing but this posture of disengagement. This is true too of faith, threatening the viability of many of our churches.

Some churches, while keeping their theology and their traditional church structures alongside a strategy of making their communications, worship, and aesthetics culturally relevant, find themselves experiencing another kind of disappearance. The church as an entity stays and even grows in size and influence. Yet, the majority of its members disappear annually to be replaced by another class of attenders. The size of the church stays the same or even grows, yet the annual turnover of attendees can run at between 60–90 percent. Such turnover may be sustainable in the short term, but one must wonder how such an approach can work long-term. Such churches are in danger of becoming what could be called flashmob churches: churches that are able to harness social networking and energy to gather an impressive crowd, but who soon disappear.

THE PURSUIT OF RELEVANCE SEEMS HELPLESS IN THE FACE OF THE NEW DISENGAGED MODE OF ATTENDING CHURCH.

The disappearing churchgoer is not just restricted to successful, contemporary megachurches. Churches of all shapes, stripes, and sizes have seen people appear one day at the back of church like apparitions—sometimes alone, sometimes in groups—then disappearing, never to be seen again and causing inexplicable peaks and troughs in attendance records. There were those who proudly proclaimed how much they loved their church and yet who were rarely around, who despite their intermittent attendance saw themselves as part of the fabric of their church. To them, regular attendance was turning up every six weeks. Then one day, as suddenly as they had luminously appeared, they disappeared. No follow-up system, no pastoral calls, and no visitor cards could stop them from disappearing again into the dark.

In such a fragile environment, how does a pastor measure their church? Was their community the five hundred who called their church home, or the maximum of two hundred and fifty who showed up on any given Sunday? A board of elders could feel elated as their services were bursting on Sunday, only to be half-empty the following week. The pursuit of relevance seems helpless in the face of this new disengaged mode of attending church. One could wonder if our "relevance" is making the problem worse.

Chapter 3

How Much More Relevant Can We Get?

HOW CHINESE ATHEISTS GET IT RIGHT

As they transitioned out of their allegiance to what they saw as the failed ideology of Communism, Chinese leaders, schooled in the art of the long-term view, looked curiously to the West to uncover the secret of her ascent from a murderous medieval backwater to a peaceful and prosperous culture. Their investigations uncovered a key factor, as an academic from China's Academy of the Social Sciences explained:

> We were asked to look into what accounted for the . . . preeminence of the West all over the world. . . . At first, we thought it was because you had more powerful guns than we had. Then we thought it was because you had the best political system. Next we focused on your economic system. But in the past twenty years, we have realized that the heart of your culture is your religion: Christianity. That is why the West has been so powerful. The Christian moral foundation of social and cultural life was what made possible . . . the successful transition to democratic politics. We don't have any doubt about this.[1]

The irony of the observation could not be thicker when you think that for half a century the Chinese, officially atheistic, persecuted religious minorities. Yet now their pragmatic vision allowed the Chinese to see the vital role that Christianity had played in producing the West's most life-giving cultural fruit.

Around the same time as China's highest official held high-level meetings to learn from the West's religious foundations, the architects of the European Union's constitution were willfully ignoring their own culture's foundations. While Europe increasingly slides into unbelief, a visit to the Continent finds one drenched in Europe's Christian past. Cathedrals, churches, charities, customs, street and city names—to step on European soil is to find a continent shaped by the Christian faith at almost a subatomic level.

Yet the draft of the 2004 European Union, while rhapsodizing about Europe's cultural roots found in the Greek philosophers and Enlightenment rationalists, ignored the region's 1,500-year Christian history. Even the atheist president of Poland, Aleksander Kwasniewski, could see the lunacy of such an omission, protesting that "there is no excuse for making reference to ancient Greece and Rome, and to the Enlightenment, without making reference to the Christian values which are so important to the development of Europe."[2]

British historian Michael Burleigh observes that the Western culture-shaping class "prefer their monopolistic mantra of 'diversity,' 'human rights,' and 'tolerance,' as if they invented them, unaware of the extent to which these are products of a deeper Christian culture based on ideas and structures that are so deeply entrenched that most of us are hardly aware of them."[3]

Thus in the West, a unique kind of culture has emerged, one that promotes elements of the universal Christian vision of justice while deconstructing the Christian tradition and any convention that attempts to limit individual freedom and autonomy.

MINISTRY TO A VERY DIFFERENT THIRD WORLD

To understand both our current cultural climate and the limitations of the relevant approach, the work of the provocative sociologist Philip Rieff is a helpful tool. Rieff divides cultures into three broad types.[4] Here are the first two:

1. The First Culture: First cultures believe in many gods. The individual is a victim to fate, and the world is full of irrational spiritual forces. To survive, the individual must obey the taboos of the gods, through turning to shaman and witch doctors for guidance and protection. The world is a frightening, spiritually charged place. The individual feels besieged by forces beyond their control.

2. The Second Culture: Second cultures are scriptural cultures, rooted in the Judeo-Christian ethic. They center their entire order on the worship of the one true God. The whole of the universe is arranged by God in a rational, sacred order. There are not taboos, but rather sacred prohibitions and commandments that must be obeyed, and these commandments and prohibitions ensure justice and human flourishing. In the second cultures, God reveals Himself through Scripture; thus religion is creedal. The individual finds peace, security, and faith by worshiping God and obeying His commands in the world.

As we have already seen, the quest for relevance in the Western evangelical church has been driven by the field of study known as missiology—the science of doing mission cross-culturally. Missionaries such as Donald McGavran and Peter Wagner returned from serving in non-Western cultures and applied what they had learned on the field to Western contexts, creating the church growth and contemporary church models. In the '90s, those who were reacting against the church growth and contemporary church models also turned to missiology, in particular Lesslie Newbigin and David Bosch—wrestling with the question, "How do we approach post-modern culture with a missiological mindset?"

Using Rieff's model, we can see that at its beginnings, missiology grew out of an interaction between second cultures taking the gospel to first cultures. It grew from the desire of missionaries from the Christian West to responsibly and faithfully evangelize pre-Christian cultures, without imposing cultural beliefs that were not central to the gospel.

Missiology taught us that if you want to communicate the gospel to a different culture, you need to find cultural bridges. You need to speak in the language of the culture to which you are communicating. Symbols and stories that resonate are essential to effective evangelism. Indigenous communities of faith thrive on the back of already-existing cultural structures. Missionaries must ask, "What elements of my Christian practice are from my home culture and not essential to the gospel? How do I avoid pushing my culture upon those I am sharing the gospel with?" The goal is to eventually see the birth of an indigenous gospel movement within that culture. Knowing this, we can see how attractive this model was to those who were trying to reach the increasingly secular West, which seemed to look less Christian each day.

MISSIOLOGY:

Communicate the gospel, using indigenous symbols, stories & structures.

1st Culture ← 2nd Culture

Avoid colonizing and forcing 2nd culture upon 1st culture.

To many, the secularizing West had begun to look like Rieff's first culture, a pre-Christian society. Therefore if we were to reach the West, we must find cultural bridges and use the stories, language, and symbols of the culture to reach it. We must ask what elements of our culture (Christian culture, or Christendom culture) we were pushing on others that they did not need. Much of this move was good. Relevance is important; it has a place. Clear communication of the gospel, in understandable language with familiar symbols and stories, is critical.

Yet we missed something crucial. Philip Rieff noted that there was another world. Our contemporary world, the West, had not reverted to a first culture. It was now something altogether different. It had become what Rieff labeled a third culture.

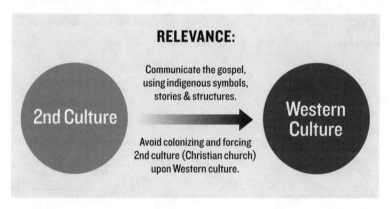

RELEVANCE:

Communicate the gospel, using indigenous symbols, stories & structures.

2nd Culture ➤ Western Culture

Avoid colonizing and forcing 2nd culture (Christian church) upon Western culture.

3. The Third Culture: Third cultures exist primarily to define themselves against second cultures. They believe in no greater truth; there is no sacred order. Instead, their energy is devoted to deconstructing the sacred. They have no creed but heresy, and their cultural power is centered on transgressing the sacred commandments and prohibitions of the second culture. The only authority is found with the individual, thus there is no possibility of a sacred order. All authority that challenges

and restricts the autonomy of the individual must be leveled. With no sacred order, the third culture is in constant flux, as new authorities and rules appear but are soon deconstructed. The meaning and purpose of all stories, rules, and symbols is contested and left up to individual interpretation.

The third culture of the West is ultimately a post–Judeo-Christian culture, not reverting to a pre-Christian paganism but rather is a culture bent on disfiguring the second culture. Rieff, who was Jewish, noted that the third culture was created by "post-Jews and post-Christians who no longer have a grip on the commanding truths."[5] They are intent on deconstructing their former faith and heritage. Therefore, the mode of the third culture is the destruction of all modes. Nothing is solid in the third culture; it is a ghostly world that corrodes anything solid. The third culture is not anarchic as such. Rather, it positions itself as the latest incarnation of the West's mission to re-educate the world. It propagates its own creed, one which believes in no creeds, except the creed of self. The third culture is the engine that powers post-Christianity. The ultimate authority in the third culture is the self.

> WITH ITS GREAT MISSION TO PROHIBIT ANYONE FROM PROHIBITING, THE THIRD CULTURE'S DOGMA IS THAT THERE SHOULD BE NO DOGMA.

The quest for relevance has been positioned on the idea that we the church as a second culture are communicating to a culture which has reverted to a first culture. However, we are dealing with a very different beast—a third culture. Missiology makes sense when you are looking for cultural bridges—symbols, signs, and stories—to communicate to a culture that is somewhat fixed and aware of its identity. Yet how do you communicate relevantly to a culture in which every story, symbol, and sign is contested, in which stories, symbols, and signs move in and out of fashion at an incredible rate?

In classic missiology, indigenous churches are able to grow like a vine on the lattice of strong, pre-existing structures like tribes, extended families, villages, and ethnic groups. But how do you achieve this in the West, which is in the process of atomizing in radical individualism, an individualism that has deconstructed binding ties and mediating institutions?

COLONIZING AND BEING COLONIZED

The danger for Christian second cultures communicating the gospel to pre-Christian cultures is that they may inadvertently colonize them. The danger when Christian second cultures communicate the gospel to post-Christian third cultures is that they themselves may be colonized—for the third culture is just as evangelistic as the second culture. With its great mission to prohibit anyone from prohibiting, it seeks to propagate its dogma that there should be no dogma.

Approaches that are purely based on an attempt at cultural relevance will ultimately fail in the face of the corrosive power of the post-Christian third culture. In the third culture, you can reach levels of blistering hipness, gain position within a key industry, hold an encyclopedic knowledge of popular culture, throw yourself into the great justice causes of the day, and still your belief in the second culture values of faith will see you viewed as beyond the pale.

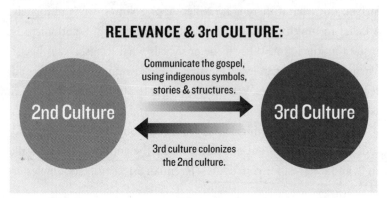

RELEVANCE & 3rd CULTURE:

2nd Culture

Communicate the gospel, using indigenous symbols, stories & structures.

3rd Culture

3rd culture colonizes the 2nd culture.

The temptation of this discomfort between orthodox Christian faith and the civil religion of the third culture is to do what it takes for the pressure to go away. All the believer must do is ease up on the beliefs that grate against contemporary sensibilities. Tweak your view on sexuality to be more embracing of today's mood, or move from a particularist view of Jesus to a universalist one, and you are warmly embraced into the fold. Thus, for many Christians raised with the ethic of relevance, of proving to the world that Christians can both be believers and carry the contemporary currency of cool, the new pressure presented by an intolerant tolerance proves too much. Some compartmentalize their beliefs into an orthodox/secularist mashup, and others simply disappear into the cold embrace of secularity.

THE DESIRE FOR A KILLER APP

Faced with such a discomforting reality, presented with our cultural challenge and our own complicity, we scramble for a solution. We are shaped by a phenomenon that journalist Evgeny Morozov[6] labels as solutionism, the largely arrogant belief that we have the resources and smarts to under our own steam solve any problem that confronts us. All we need to do is discover the Killer App, and the discomfort we feel, the obstacles we face, will disappear. We just need that program, that new expression of church shape, the silver bullet to defeat secularism. But what if there is no Killer App? Solutionism is ultimately a belief in novelty, and a lack of patience and faith. Solutionism is instant gratification. What if the answer is what it has always been? The path of walking in Jesus' footsteps, of following the traditions and teaching of the apostles. What if the answer to our culture's challenges is still the gospel?

In the book of Jeremiah, God proclaims, "Stand by the roads, and look, and ask for the ancient paths, where the good way is; and walk in it, and find rest for your souls" (Jeremiah 6:16 ESV). God invites us to follow the ancient paths. A path is not a Killer App. It is a process. An instant solution requires no faith, because the problem is resolved in a moment. In contrast a path requires faith, and courage. Thus we understand why one of Jesus' most consistent encouragements to those who followed Him was to have courage.

CREATIVE MINORITY

In Scripture when the people of God found themselves surrounded by more powerful nations, sent into exile to live amongst the Babylonians, or tempted to abandon the ways of Yahweh and submit to the idols of the nations, God would send His prophets. They would remind Israel of her faith in the one true God, of the futility of the idol worship of the nations, and their calling to be a holy, righteous, and just people. In 2013, in New York, a group of Christian leaders anxious to negotiate the new cultural landscape gathered to listen to the advice of a contemporary Hebrew prophet, in the form of Rabbi Jonathan Sacks, the former Chief Rabbi of the UK and Commonwealth.

Sacks captured the sense that something fundamental was occurring within Western culture, noting that "there are moments in history, and we are living through one now, when something new is taking shape but we do not know precisely what."[7] For Sacks, an incisive observer of contemporary culture, this new moment was shaped by a crisis within Western culture, a crisis of which "the results lie all around us: the collapse of marriage, the fracturing of the family, the fraying of the social bond, the partisanship of politics at a time when national interest demands something larger, the loss of trust in public institutions, the buildup of debt whose burden will fall on future generations, and the failure of a shared morality to lift us out of the morass of individualism, hedonism, consumerism, and relativism. We know these things, yet we seem collectively powerless to move beyond them."[8]

In such a confronting cultural moment, we must ask, according to Sacks, "Can civilizational decline be arrested? To which the great prophetic answer is 'Yes.' For the prophets taught us that after every exile there is a return, after every destruction the ruins can be rebuilt, after every crisis there can be a rebirth, if—if we have faith in God's faith in us."[9] This cultural rebirth occurs in what historian Arnold Toynbee labeled "creative minorities."[10] For Sacks, the people of God exiled in Babylon are an example of a creative minority—who, despite being in exile and surrounded by a more powerful and often hostile culture, are commanded by God to

> Build houses and settle down; plant gardens and eat what they produce. Marry and have sons and daughters; find wives for your sons and give your daughters in marriage, so that they too may have sons and daughters. Increase in number there; do not decrease. Also, seek the peace and prosperity of the city to which I have carried you into exile. Pray to the Lord for it, because if it prospers, you too will prosper. (Jeremiah 29:5–7 NIV)

Creative minorities find themselves withdrawn and distant from what they know and find comfort in. This distance enables them to see the myths and blind spots of their own culture, to reject these myths, and find a greater dependency in God. This dependency on a source of power and truth outside of the dominant culture leads creative minorities to refresh and reinvigorate ailing cultures.

To be a creative minority is to live with a creative tension, as Sacks explains: "To become a creative minority. . . is not easy, because it involves maintaining strong links with the outside world while staying true to your faith, seeking not merely to keep the sacred flame burning but also to transform the larger society of which you are a part."[11] Much of the strategy of relevance, whether consciously or subconsciously, has been built upon reducing the tension many believers feel with the wider culture. However, to be a creative minority, Sacks warns, "It isn't easy. . . . It isn't for the faint-hearted. But it is creative."[12] Toynbee noted that creative minorities are formed by this tension, which he labeled Withdraw/Return, describing the way that minorities must withdraw from their culture to return with healing truth.

Toynbee noted that Jesus' ministry, and especially His death and resurrection, was the ultimate example of Withdraw/Return. The gospel invites us into the process of withdrawal-return, to place everything at the foot of the cross, to withdraw into the presence of God, submitting ourselves to His lordship, repenting of the ways in which we have rebelled. We then emerge washed by grace as a new creation, charged to bring the healing truth of the gospel to the nations. Yet in the third culture of the West, in the beautiful culture that surrounds us, there is another gospel that competes for our allegiance.

THE GNOSTIC TEMPTATION

After encouraging the creative minority of Jews living in Babylon to seek the peace and prosperity of the pagan city in which they found themselves exiled, God warns His people, "Do not let the prophets and diviners among you deceive you. Do not listen to the dreams you encourage them to have. They are prophesying lies to you in my name. I have not sent them" (Jeremiah 29:8–9 NIV). The creative minority would face the temptation to abandon their godly calling. This temptation would come in a religious form, cloaked in dreams and lies. For those wishing again to be a creative minority in our time, we also face a similar temptation, wrapped in spiritual language, reshaping our dreams with lies.

Over half a century ago another contemporary Hebrew prophet warned of another temptation faced by Western culture. The philosopher Martin Buber, discerning an emerging and destructive trajectory within society, warned that a new religion was being proclaimed.[13] Warning both his fellow Jews as well as Christians, Buber observed that this new religion was fundamentally different from biblical faith. This new religion could be detected in an increasing obsession with the self, with personal development and the preference of spirituality over religion, and with therapy over communion with a transcendent God. It was the elevation of self above God. Although this religion seemed new, Buber noted it was the return of an older strain of thought. It was the return of Gnosticism—the gospel of self.

Chapter 4

The Gospel of Self (Gnosticism)

*George Orwell introduced the dictator Big Brother in his novel 1984
. . . But now . . . Big Brother is all too famous, and all too obvious. If
Big Brother were to appear before us now, we'd point to him and say,
"Watch out! He's Big Brother!" There's no longer any place for a Big
Brother in this real world of ours. Instead these so-called Little People
have come on the scene . . . they seem to be steadily undermining us.*

Haruki Murakami, *1Q84*

FROM SALVATION TO SAFE

Critics note that each year Todd Haynes's 1995 film *SAFE* appears to
grow more relevant. *SAFE* tells the story of Carol, a Southern California housewife played by Julianne Moore who appears to have it all.
She has a wealthy husband and a large, well-furnished house. She is
attractive, is surrounded by friends, and spends her days working out
at the gym, shopping for furniture, and being pampered at the beauty
salon. However, after an allergic reaction, and a panic attack in her
car while driving, Carol begins to develop a terrifying fear that she is

facing a battle against a hidden enemy that seems to be attacking her well-being. There are significant parallels between *SAFE* and many of Alfred Hitchcock's thrillers, which feature a beautiful woman who is wrenched from the comfort of her ordinary life and traumatized by a dangerous assailant. However, in *SAFE* the assailant is unseen. At a children's party in front of her friends, Carol again has a terrifying panic attack, which leads her to attend a seminar about toxins, chemicals, and stress. For Carol, the seminar is a conversion experience, in which she comes to believe that her assailant is the modern world.

The facilitator of the seminar encourages the audience to find their "safe place," a refuge in their home, which is free from contemporary contaminants. This advice sends Carol on an obsessive quest to rid herself of toxins. Despite her doctor and a psychiatrist finding nothing wrong with her, she eventually makes the decision to relocate to a secluded community in the desert, which brands itself as a safe place free from contamination. Despite the desert commune's being more akin to a kind of cult run by a HIV-positive guru who blames his followers' weakness for their suffering, Carol begins to feel safe. That is, until a nature walk, where Carol unintentionally happens upon a highway and is exposed to exhaust fumes. Carol demands a room farther from the road, but no room is available apart from a completely sealed, igloo-like structure built by one of the more obsessive residents of the commune.

In the movie's final scene, Carol bids farewell to her husband and son and retreats into the sealed igloo. Now utterly sealed off from the outside world, she stands alone and, following the advice of one of the commune's leaders, she stands in the austerity of the igloo in front of the mirror and pathetically repeats to her reflection, "I love you . . . I really love you . . . I love you." She has finally found her safe place. Yet she is falling apart, cut off from human relationships. As the movie ended with Carol staring into the mirror a broken woman, I could not but help think of C. S. Lewis's work *The Great Divorce*. Lewis imagines hell as a boring English town, populated by souls unaware of their own damnation who, in their attempts to find autonomy and freedom, move further away from each other, pushing individualism all the way to utter isolation, disappearing into Narcissus's pool of self-obsession.

SAFE is essentially a religious work, albeit one shaped by our contemporary attitudes. The film follows a classical Christian narrative, yet one that is emptied of its theological content. Carol, despite being wealthy and privileged, is confronted by her spiritual poverty. This existential crisis is never recognized as such, and thus her cosmic smallness and fragility does not lead her on an existential quest for salvation. Her deeply materialist worldview leads her not to reflect and ponder life's great questions, but instead her spiritual crisis is focused purely upon the body. She wonders why her skin reacts, why she feels overwhelmed by exhaust fumes, why the chemicals at the beauty salon cause her nosebleeds.

In the traditional Christian narrative, an individual confronted by their own spiritual poverty would be forced to examine their own sinfulness and egotism. However, in *SAFE* the caustic and destructive effects of sin are reduced into the material substance of toxins. In the Christian narrative, the individual who is made aware of their own spiritual poverty and their own sinfulness is then made aware of their need of salvation. In *SAFE* Carol, after being made aware of her own physical fragility and chemical intoxication, seeks the secular version of salvation; safety. Carol's conversion occurs during a sermon-like presentation on the toxicity of the contemporary world, and she feels that she has become enlightened to the true nature of the world. She will be whole when she is safe.

In the established Christian spiritual journey, the individual, having undergone conversion, seeks out spiritual community and fellowship. Carol does just that, as she relocates to her desert commune safe place. The parallels between the desert commune and a monastery are striking. The group lives austere lives, shorn of the toxic nasties of contemporary life. They sing together, listen to teachings from their guru, and retreat to their cell-like rooms. Eventually, like a modern-day version of the medieval writer and nun Julian of Norwich, Carol seals herself into her igloo-like cell. However, unlike Julian, who encountered a transcendent God in prayer and Scripture, Carol can only search inward for love, seeking an answer to her spiritual poverty in her own resources. Thus the final scene of *SAFE* is a devastating piece of cinema, as a broken and spiritually impoverished Carol feebly utters into the mirror her mantra of self-love, and her quest to find love, truth, and peace within collapses into an anxious, miserable heap.

THE SELF RUN WILD

SAFE is a brilliant examination of the quest for love and meaning in the third culture. For when we observe the third culture with clear eyes, underneath its corrosive nature and attacks upon any dogma we see what the culture truly believes in. Theologian David Bentley Hart notes:

> Our age is not one in danger of reverting to paganism. . . . If we turn from Christ today, we turn only towards the god of absolute will. . . . A . . . retreat to the old gods is not possible for us; we can find no shelter there, nor can we sink away gently into those old illusions and tragic consolations that Christ exposed as falsehoods. To love or be nourished by the gods, we would have to fear them.[1]

Hart's point is a powerful one: For a genuine return to the paganism of the first culture, one would have to seriously argue a scenario that would see huge swaths of contemporary Westerners willing to lay down and surrender their wills, possessions, and autonomy at the foot of Mars or Apollo. Hart writes:

> *The Christian God has taken up everything into himself; all the treasures of ancient wisdom, all the splendor of creation, every good thing has been assumed into the story of the incarnate God, and every stirring towards transcendence is soon recognized by the modern mind—weary of God—as leading back toward faith . . . The only cult that can truly thrive in the aftermath of Christianity is a narrow service of the self, of the impulses of the will, of the nothingness that is all the withdrawal of Christianity leaves behind.[2]*

The only authority left then in the third culture is the authority of the self. The mythology of contemporary Western culture tells a story in which humanity is moving away from the superstitions of the past into a more evolved, intelligent future. However, that great observer of cultural change, Tom Wolfe, in a 1976 article entitled "The Me Decade," noted, like Martin Buber, that Western culture was not moving forward but reaching back to an older stream of thought. Reflecting on all of the various streams of individualism breaking out, Wolfe wrote, "In one form or another they arrive at an axiom first propounded by the Gnostic Christians some 1,800 years ago."[3] Wolfe traced the outbreak of the religion of Me, with its fear of commitment and desire to discover a shiny vision of the future for the self, back to the ancient Christian heresy of Gnosticism.

> GNOSTICISM IS AN ATTEMPT TO RETAIN THE FRUITS OF CHRISTIANITY AND THE SOLACE OF FAITH WHILE MAXIMIZING THE INDIVIDUAL'S AUTHORITY.

Gnosticism was a spiritual viewpoint that emerged sometime in the first century. It is multi-formed and complex. Because of its anti-creedal nature, it is fluid. Gnosticism thus stole from all of the religions that surrounded it, combining parts of pagan belief, Persian religions, Judaism, Christianity, and Greek philosophy to create a hodgepodge spirituality. Yet there are key basic beliefs of Gnosticism.

The world of time, space, and matter in which we live is inferior.

The world is inferior because it has been created by an inferior and possibly evil god.

Beyond our world and the inferior god, there is a sublime place to which we must progress.

We can progress to the sublime place when we discover the divine spark within ourselves.

Truth is found within the individual. We must look inside to find our true self.

We can under our own steam progress to the sublime place through knowledge (in the Greek, "gnosis"). We escape the inferior world by finding the hidden pieces of knowledge in the world and in ourselves.

Essentially Gnosticism is an inversion of the gospel, yet it is a heresy that follows Christian faith like a parasite. Roger Lundin writes:

No heresy has proved more stubbornly resilient than gnosticism. In the early centuries of the Christian age, gnosticism struggled with orthodoxy for the very soul of the faith. In later centuries, up through the modern age, the gnostic impulse has repeatedly resurfaced in church and culture . . . the gnostic viewpoint has always posed a threat and remained a temptation to orthodoxy. And in the past two hundred years, it has reemerged as a dominant intellectual and cultural force, even as the public influence of Christianity has waned.[4]

The constant temptation of Gnosticism reminds us that the problem with the Western culture is not unbelief, but in Ross Douthat's words, "Bad religion: the slow-motion collapse of traditional Christianity and the rise of a variety of destructive pseudo-Christianities in its place."[5] Gnosticism is such a pseudo-Christianity. Essentially, forms of Christian Gnosticism attempted to reshape Christian belief, taking its concepts, language, and texts and turning them into something new. Eric Voegelin observed that the Gnostic heresy would spring up parasitically, in times when cultural Christianity grew alongside devoted faith, and cultural Christians wished for a version of belief that was less dependent upon faith and submission and more on the individual's personal control. Gnosticism is an attempt to retain the fruits of Christianity and the solace of faith while maximizing the individual's authority. It is the post-Christian impulse par excellence.

There are key elements that most experts attribute to Gnosticism.

1) ALL HAIL ME

The individual in the Gnostic understanding was not a child of God, but rather contained the potential to become a god. Gnosticism moved authority from the seat of God to the seat of the human soul. Each of us was filled with potential, a divine spark; we just need to look within to uncover the god, the star within us. The trajectory of Christianity, the story of the gospel, was reversed. The perfect and all-powerful God did not descend to earth and give us the gift of salvation. Instead, the individual soul, filled with potential and power, must ascend to the heights of perfection, powered by its own smarts. The Gnostic soul must create and shape itself, becoming the author of its own identity. The Gnostic self then becomes the seat of all authority, the main actor in its own personal cosmic drama.

2) INFERIOR WORLD, INFERIOR GOD

The Gnostics saw the world we inhabit as inferior, a kind of half-botched copy of a much more beautiful and perfect world that existed elsewhere. This botched world in which we live was the creation of a limited god. The world is inferior because it was created by an inferior god, thus this world is a world of darkness, which explains the phenomenon of evil. The evil in the world is not therefore attributed to the sinful heart of humans, but rather the shoddy workmanship of the inferior god. Salvation is found in escaping this world for a beautiful, perfect place—which is definitely not where we are. The inferior god did not deserve worship, or faith, or obedience. When the inferior god created our world, kinds of divine sparks were left within the world hidden in forms of secret knowledge (Gnosis in the Greek, hence the title Gnosticism). The means of escaping the world could be found by discovering the spark of divinity within humans, discovering the secret knowledge in the world, and becoming enlightened.

3) FLEE!

The Gnostic understanding of the world turns Genesis upside down. No longer is the world of God's good creation blighted by human sin; yet it still contains His hand, His order, and His presence. In the Gnostic vision whatever order seems to exist in the world is flawed and must be escaped or reshaped by human hands. The natural order of the world is too compromised, too dirty, and too ordinary for the Gnostic soul to be involved in; they must flee. Any definition that defines or binds the self must be rejected, therefore the Gnostics wished to escape their bodies and to move beyond being defined by a gender. The consequences and realities of this world must be avoided. Hell for the Gnostic is being stuck on earth within this created order.

Some Gnostics saw that the inferior god, in his imperfection and possibly his malice, created boundaries to keep us from escaping the world. The Gnostic then must gain secret knowledge with which to break past these boundaries. Gnostic spirituality then is not one of obedience and faith but rather of breaking boundaries, rejecting definitions, and transgressing limits. Answers are to be found within. The great quest of life is to discover who you really are—to ignore what those around you say, break past the barriers and definitions and rules placed around you, and flout any external authority. To look inside, find your true self, and self-create.

CONTEMPORARY GNOSTICISM

Many today no longer hold to the more transcendent forms of Gnosticism that see the soul being freed by death to continue its cosmic journey of self-discovering. Instead, contemporary Gnosticism is more reduced, more earthbound, yet the basic schema is the same. While the early Gnostics wished to escape the world of matter to enter a purely spiritual plane, the reduced neo-Gnosticism of our day wishes to escape the world of the mundane for the world of the awesome, the stimulating, and the pleasurable. Because the early Gnostics saw matter as evil, not only did they want to escape the world, they wanted to escape their bodies, to be perfected spiritual beings. This seems at odds with our body-obsessed culture of today—or is it? Our contemporary Gnosticism wishes to escape our real bodies to become perfected bodies. Through our own efforts, we can smash through the barriers and find happiness through attaining the perfect bodies we see in the imagery all around us.

None of the writers who point to the influence of Gnosticism on our current religious and cultural landscape make the claim that a continuous movement of Gnosticism has existed in the West that connects to its beginnings in the first century. It is not so much a movement as a temptation, one whose origins begin in the garden with the whispered promise of the serpent that humans "may be like God" through a rebellion of transgression and autonomy that shatters the God-ordained order. Gnosticism is a term for the trajectory of humans to flee from God, His order, and His authority. As theologian Hans Urs von Balthasar writes when dealing with Gnosticism, "When we look more closely, we can see that we are dealing with a confrontation which has never ended and is constantly assuming new forms."[6]

Von Balthasar saw Gnosticism as implicit in Eastern religions, the contemporary New Age movement, and much of the German philosophy that so influenced the contemporary Western mind. Political scientist Eric Voegelin wrote of Gnosticism's influence on the political systems of both the left and right, which desired to move beyond God and longed for the present order to be destroyed, which desired for society to find salvation through human effort and knowledge (gnosis) alone, which drags the world into perfection. James A. Herrick has shown the Gnostic origins of the new religious synthesis popularized by such celebrities as Oprah Winfrey.

Carl Jung, whose influence on both psychology and the self-development movement cannot be overstated, openly declared his Gnostic influences, to the point of claiming that his writings were the direct words of a second-century Egyptian Gnostic who would use Jung's body as a channel.[7] The Gnostic contours of humanistic psychology are quite evident. Another giant of psychology, Abraham Maslow, is well known for his concept of self-actualization, which reflects many Gnostic ideas. The individual finds himself in a conformist world from which he must escape and find the fulfilled person within. Through the acquiring of knowledge and techniques, the individual can break from the limits that hold him back, and become self-actualized.[8] We cannot change the surrounding culture; we can only change ourselves. We can achieve self-mastery while conquering our failings and our sins, all without God. This is not only the kernel of Maslow's teaching; it is the foundation of most self-help thinking and the human potential movements that have so shaped the modern self.

GNOSTICISM AS THE GREAT POST-CHRISTIAN RELIGION OF THE THIRD CULTURE

One thinker who is explicit about their embrace of Gnosticism is the American cultural critic Harold Bloom. Bloom did not point out the Gnostic roots of one segment of contemporary life or another; rather he argued that we should all quit the pretending, because Gnosticism has won. Bloom claimed not only that we should accept this fact, but that it was a good thing. Bloom advocated the adoption of Gnosticism as the post-Christian religion par excellence. There is so much that Bloom gets wrong in his book *The American Religion: The Emergence of the Post-Christian Nation*, but at some points his words make us worry that he may get some things right. Speaking of faith in the West, Bloom charges,

> Mormons, and Southern Baptists . . . Methodists, Roman Catholics, and even Jews and Muslims are . . . more Gnostic than normative in their deepest and unwariest beliefs. . . . Even our secularists, indeed even our professed atheists, are more Gnostic than humanist in their ultimate presuppositions. We are a religiously mad culture, furiously searching for the spirit, but each of us is subject and object of the one quest, which must be for the original self.[9]

Just when it is too painful, Bloom sticks the knife in further:

> Ancient Gnosticism was an elite religion. . . . The oddity of our . . . Gnosis is that it is a mass phenomenon. There are tens of millions . . . whose obsessive idea of spiritual freedom violates the normative basis

*of historical Christianity, though they are incapable of realizing how
little they share of what once was considered Christian doctrine.*[10]

As the expansive scope of the Gnostic temptation is revealed,
Bloom focuses our attention upon the way that the Gnostic schema
can even write itself over other religions, in particular Christianity.
We see in Bloom's provocative statements the way that the powerful
undercurrent of Gnosticism in the West, with its religion of the self,
can influence believers without their realizing that they operate under a different kind of code than the one that they profess.

> THE CHURCH IS
> NOT DESTROYED;
> RATHER IT IS EMPTIED
> OF ITS ESSENTIAL
> TRUTHS, BECOMES
> A MERE SHADOW,
> AND EVENTUALLY
> DISAPPEARS.

Bloom's intuitive observation squares with
the research of Christian Smith and Melinda
Lundquist Denton who, after interviewing
thousands of American teenagers, found that
despite the religious or non-religious affilia-
tion of their respondents, almost all held to a
kind of loose, non-binding belief in a distant
God. A belief that does not call the individual to account, but rather believes that "the
central goal of life is to be happy and to feel
good about oneself."[11] Thus the driving belief
that truth is found within, that external sources of truth and authority must be refused, that our path to salvation is self-powered, over-
comes Christianity not by siege but by infiltration from within. The
church is not destroyed; rather it is emptied of its essential truths,
becomes a mere shadow, and eventually disappears. In the same way,
believers who are emptied of the essential truths of orthodox Christianity, who find themselves walking in step with the Gnostic tune of
the day, find themselves becoming more spectral as their faith slowly
disappears.

ANCIENT GNOSTICISM	CONTEMPORARY GNOSTICISM	THE GOSPEL
The world is inferior.	Your world is inferior.	Creation is good, although broken by the fall. Yet Christ has won victory, and creation now groans for the day heaven and earth will be reunited.
Matter is the problem.	The mundane is the problem.	Sin and rebellion against God and His created order is the problem.
Escape from your body to perfect-spirit.	Turn your body into a perfect-looking body.	Jesus' gift of grace frees us from sin and death.
Look inward to find truth and the god within.	Look inward to find the real you.	God's revelation opens our eyes to God and the true nature of things.
Escape the world to the perfect spiritual place.	Escape the mundane to the amazing life.	Joy and meaning is found in worshiping and serving God.
Move toward perfection through finding hidden spiritual knowledge.	Move toward the perfect life through tips, tweaks, hacks, and the secrets of success. Self-create.	Pursue Christlikeness.
You are a seeker, pursuing spiritual truths and hidden knowledge.	You are a seeker, pursuing fulfillment through incredible experiences and pleasure.	You are a recipient of Grace. Pursued and loved by God.
Move past the inferior god to find the real God beyond.	Move past organized religion, and find spirituality.	God chooses to partner with us in His mission in the world through the church. The church is a foretaste of the coming kingdom. Build up the church.
Move toward fulfillment by breaking past the barriers left by the inferior god.	Move toward fulfillment by breaking past the barriers set by tradition, religion, and others.	Move toward spiritual maturity through battling against the flesh. Gain wisdom.
You are a god.	It's all about you.	It's all about God.

PART 2

LEARNING GOSPEL RESILIENCE

Chapter 5

An Exciting Opportunity

THE OPPORTUNITY THAT THE THIRD CULTURE BRINGS

It is easy to lose hope.

The church in its history has faced persecution, martyrdom, and heresy. It has outlasted empires, cultures, nations, and kingdoms. For as the Scriptures proclaim, "The gates of hell shall not prevail against it" (Matthew 16:18 ESV). Other translations use "overpower." It is easy to forget this as we face the challenges of our day. Confronted with our post-Christian culture, with its Gnostic view of the world, one can lose hope. A cursory glance at history notes that when the church faces new social contexts and challenges, there is much angst. Yet opportunities arise for a new engagement between orthodox, historical faith and new cultural landscapes.

I sit here writing in an area of Melbourne, Australia, first evangelized over a century ago by Methodist missionaries on horseback. This evangelistic effort was part of a global expansion of the gospel, which church historian John Wolffe notes occurred in the midst of a "context of rapidly changing societies, experiencing very considerable stresses due to major population growth, migration, industrialization and radical political change. Against this background the religious world too was in a state of flux, adapting to the challenges and opportunities brought by the formal ending of established churches in the United States, the inability of the established churches to meet all the spiritual needs of the people of Britain, and the failure convincingly to export the Anglican establishment to Britain's burgeoning colonies."[1]

The church faced a new and confusing culture, a world in the midst of incredible change and transformation. Despite these challenges, the response of the church would birth many of the giants upon whose shoulders we stand. Emerging into this new and challenging environment would be incredible movements including Methodism, Abolitionism, the Salvation Army, and the Clapham Sect. It would see the rise of leaders such as John Wesley, Charles Spurgeon, William Wilberforce, Hannah More, and George Whitefield. It would be a new global movement led by a ragtag bunch of characters: ex-slaves, indigenous leaders, activists, and wealthy philanthropists. It is a story that has been repeated throughout the history of the church: when new social landscapes emerge, no matter how challenging they may be, they present an opportunity for the church to flourish, and with the leading of the Holy Spirit, for it to birth new movements, leaders, churches, and creative minorities.

New Cultural Landscapes + Faithful Orthodoxy + Courageous Creative Response = Revitalization of the Church and Culture

The third culture in which we live is a new and daunting social landscape, a changing environment that requires us to look anew at the context into which God has called us to serve, minister, and do mission. The challenge we face offers us the chance to again enter the place of pressure and challenge, which pushes us to new and vibrant forms of orthodox faith—to embrace the tension at the heart of being part of a creative minority.

CREATIVE MINORITIES: GOING DEEP

Recently, I watched a documentary that explored the diversity of teeming life in the deepest and most remote jungles. We are shown the incredible response of the jungle to the falling of a tree. We see the open space created when a huge tree falls in the dense jungle. Instantly, a race begins among the plant life to fill the space. Light pours in and space opens up to be filled. The space where the tree once stood is filmed for months using time-lapse photography. The space is quickly filled with a variety of broad-leafed plants; their large leaves are able to capture large amounts of sunlight, ensuring rapid and spectacular growth.

Soon thin trees begin to break through the broad-leafed plants, shooting their wispy trunks up into the unoccupied space, beginning to fill their branches with leaves. The growth of these trees seems impressive compared to the broad-leafed plants around, yet next to the giant trunks of the large trees that surround them, their height is not that impressive. In reality, their position is precarious, for soon something begins to happen around their thin and vulnerable trunks. Small, thin vines begin to lap at the bottom of their trunks, snaking their way up. At first there are just a few vines, but soon they are legion and, piggybacking off the preexisting structures of the thin trees, they soon dominate the space and the sunlight. The thin trees now are almost invisible, buckling under a suffocating blanket of vines. The vines appear to have won the race.

For a while there is nothing, just the vines. The growth appears to have halted, but then something magnificent happens. A lone trunk appears seemingly from nowhere, piercing the blanket of vines. Its trunk is thicker, its form solid. Rising above the vines, it keeps moving, at first doubling the height of the other trees and plants competing for the open space. Soon, it is ten times their height. Before long it has reached the height of the surrounding trees. It is a gigantic, magnificent tree. The space has now been filled. This tree will last for centuries.

> JUST LIKE A HUGE TREE, CREATIVE MINORITIES ARE BUILT ON DEEP ROOTS.

The broad-leafed plants that initially fill the space do so by gaining spectacular, visible early results. Yet their leaves, roots, and structure are fragile. They sacrifice sustainability and longevity for short-term gain. The trees that break through next also gain some success, but their structure, too, is not resilient. The vines gain some success at the expense of others. They parasitically exist on the hard work of surrounding structures, only to eventually overwhelm them. All of these strategies do not succeed.

When it comes to doing ministry and mission, in the open space created by the disappearing church in the third culture, we can face similar temptations. We can create something that is spectacular and visible, but ultimately fragile. We can attempt to grow quick at the expense of long-term sustainability. We can parasitically live off pre-existing structures, eventually overwhelming them with our critique, with their collapse being our collapse. For just like the huge tree, creative minorities are built upon deep roots.

FROM RELEVANCE TO REBUILDING

The huge tree wins the race by doing something counterintuitive. While the others fight for space, air, and light, it goes underground. While the others head upwards pushing through the surface, it goes deep. While the others pursue visibility at the expense of stability, the tree remains underground, hidden, building powerful roots. The deep underground foundations grown by the tree ensure that it is connected to deep and unseen sources of water, nutrients, and life. Once these are secured, growth can then happen. The tree is willing to lose the initial battles in order to win the war.

In the third culture, which corrodes and seduces us, which erodes commitments, faith, and covenant, we need to be like the tree. The response to a culture built on superficiality, which reduces the world to a shallow secularity, is depth. We need sources of life and sustenance not found in the adulation or respect of the public. In the third culture which rips at roots, which tears at foundations, we need depth, we need roots, and we need foundations. As churches, we need to move to a strategy of rebuilding.

At the beginning of His ministry, Jesus at the synagogue reads from Isaiah that "the Spirit of the Lord God is upon Me, because the Lord has anointed Me to bring good news to the poor" (Isaiah 61:1), pointing the scripture to Himself by announcing that in Him this messianic promise is being revealed. The audience would have understood that following in the wake of this messianic leader and His ministry would be people who are described as righteous trees, planted by the Lord to glorify Him. Isaiah writes of these followers of the Messiah,

They will rebuild
The ancient ruins
They will restore
The former devastations
They will renew the
Ruined cities, the devastations
of many generations.
(Isaiah 61:4)

We as followers of the Messiah Jesus, living within the time of His kingdom rule, now must take up the mantle of being rebuilders. We face a cultural landscape, inner private worlds, devastated and depleted by the pursuit of unlimited autonomy. This pursuit has seen churches and believers disappear. Thus, we need again to rebuild the devastated spaces and structures of our culture; we need to breathe commitment, responsibility, and dedication back into our faith and our churches. Richard Foster once said, "The desperate need today is not for a greater number of intelligent people, or gifted people, but for deep people."[2] The deep roots and foundations in Christ of creative minorities will ensure resilience.

CREATIVE MINORITIES: STAYING RESILIENT

In the same documentary, we are taken to a cave deep in the jungle. Being dark and subterranean, caves are usually not the most inviting places for life; however, the particular cave filmed in the series was even more inhospitable to life—it was a cave through which ran not water but highly corrosive acid. David Attenborough, the narrator of the series, notes that one would think that in such a caustic, dark environment, no life forms could live. However, they do, and in such a potentially deadly environment certain life forms not only survive, but thrive. Such creatures are known as extremeophiles. The term covers a wide degree of species that are able to exist in extreme temperatures, live at great depth of sea, and exist in arid deserts. They have the ability to withstand huge environmental pressure and flourish. As I watched the series, the term "extremeophiles" clicked with me; it captured a kind of disciple that I knew was needed in the third culture.

Researcher Margaret Wheatley discovered that even in the most dysfunctional and toxic of workplaces and environments, a certain kind of person and leader could be found.[3] These people were not affected by their environments. Wheatley noted that their ability to thrive in caustic environments was linked to their ability to find a sense of meaning outside of their environment. Creative minorities therefore not only survive but learn to thrive in hostile environments. In a caustic, corrosive third culture, which causes us to question and doubt our commitments, we need extremeophile disciples—disciples who are resilient. In the third culture, relevance must be matched by resilience. Deep roots and foundations will ensure resilience. For as Psalm 1:3 reminds us, the faithful believer

> *Is like a tree planted beside streams of water*
> *that bears its fruit in season*
> *and whose leaf does not wither.*
> *Whatever he does prospers.*

Yet we are so used to the primacy of the individual and our seemingly inexhaustible belief that our desires are within our reach that we can fail to see just how illogical our faith in self is when held alongside our culture's supposed sensible, non-superstitious secularism. While in the popular imagination the rise of science and Enlightenment thinking in the West has delivered a beating to religion, sociologist Warren Susman[4] reminds us that our concept of self should have taken an incredible beating as well. Over the last several centuries individuals have been told that they are simply cosmic accidents, adrift on a planet on the edge of an empty universe, that we cannot even control our own emotions, that what we think of as our original thoughts, experiences, and feelings are nothing of the kind, that our motivations, interests, and desires are simply programmed into us as biological instincts.

> TO BE SHAPED BY GRACE IN A CULTURE OF SELF, THE MOST COUNTERCULTURAL ACT ONE CAN COMMIT IN THE THIRD CULTURE IS TO BREAK ITS ONLY TABOO: TO COMMIT SELF-DISOBEDIENCE.

Alongside this rather depressing picture of our humanity, we hold to what can only be described as a religious faith in our individual selves. In Galatians 1:6 Paul writes, "I am amazed that you are so quickly turning away from Him who called you by the grace of Christ and are turning to a different gospel." We face a similar fight today as we are confronted by a gospel other than the gospel of the grace of Christ; we face the gospel of self.

To be shaped by grace in a culture of self, the most countercultural act one can commit in the third culture is to break its only taboo: to commit self-disobedience. To acknowledge that authority does not lie with us, that we ultimately have no autonomy. To admit that we are broken, that we are rebellious against God and His rule. To admit that Christ is ruler. To abandon our rule and to collapse into His arms of grace. To dig deep roots into His love. We don't just need resilience; we need gospel resilience. We need relevance and clear communication, but in communicating and living out the gospel in the third culture of the West, we need resilience, the kind that can only come from a life rooted in Jesus' sacrificial gift of grace. Yet our age resists the concept of grace.

CREATIVE MINORITIES ARE BUILT ON GRACE

Grace is an unmerited gift given, sweeping the receiver off their feet. I have seen in my life several times people given unexpected gifts that have stunned them. A young migrant in a new country, cruelly swindled, having the money she lost replaced by the member of a local church. A young student who needed a car but couldn't afford one having a set of keys given to her suddenly in the middle of a Bible study. A person whose shoes were falling apart, who was given the new pair of shoes that their seminary classmate was wearing. That classmate walked home barefoot. Acts of grace. Unmerited, unexpected gift-giving. People's bodies almost double up, their eyes well with tears, their mouths drop open, and they struggle to find words to express their gratitude.

Grace is covenantal. It creates a unique kind of authority structure in which the receiver of grace is indebted to the giver of grace. That is why often people who receive an unmerited gift protest, "I simply can't take this gift," because we intuitively understand that we are indebted. Yet this is a kind of authority that is not rooted in domination, but love. The Hungarian Christian philosopher Thomas Molnar noted that Western culture, averse to any form of authority, lost sight of the vital truth that authority can be a form of love.[5] In Jesus' gift of grace, we see this truth exemplified, the marrying of love and authority. The recipients of grace find themselves taking a different posture to life. They understand themselves not as Gnostic seekers, but slaves of Christ.

Chapter 6

Reject the Implicit Prosperity Gospel. We Are Slaves, not Seekers.

FROM SEEKERS TO SLAVES OF CHRIST

A church that is no longer disappearing is the one that leads people into realizing that they are not God. The gospel proclaims that Jesus is King. The great problem is that we as good, twenty-first-century citizens of democracy don't like kings. The English chopped off the head of Charles I and established a republic under the Puritan Oliver Cromwell. The French also beheaded their King Louis XVI. The Russian Czar Nicholas died in a hail of bullets, while his young children were shot and kicked to death to prevent the royal line from continuing. The United States fought a revolutionary war so as not to be under the dominion of King George. Having shot, beheaded, and sent our sovereigns packing, today we have a soft spot for royals, but only as memories of a forgotten world. We like the royals who turn up to cut ribbons at hospital openings or have grand weddings. We tolerate them now that they have no control over us. We prefer democracy, yet God is still King. Yes, there have been many tyrant kings; however, Christ is the good King. His coronation upon the cross shows us that

He is the sacrificial servant-King of the upside-down kingdom.

N. T. Wright notes in his book *How God Became King*[1] that even among good Christians our anti-royal, democratic heritage makes the idea of living under a King hard to stomach. Often as believers we wish for the kingdom, but do not want to acknowledge the authority of the King, for at the heart of kingship is the concept of authority. Authority is the surrendering of autonomy, absolute freedom, and free choice to someone else.

Throughout history, human cultures have understood well the idea and purpose of authority. As Adam Seligman explains, "We accept the authority of those wielding power because over the long run it is in our interest to do so." So we submit ourselves to a strict and rude driving instructor for a series of lessons because we value the ultimate goal of gaining our driver's license. However, Seligman adds that contemporary Western culture "is inherently hostile to the idea and experience of authority."[2] Thus the third culture presents a mirage where we can seemingly have ultimate value without submitting to the authority of anyone, and our worlds are split in two. Our ability to shape and keep shaping a materially beautiful world, filled with options and experiences, deceives us into thinking that we have more authority than we do. As David Koyzis reminds us:

> The human capacity for adapting the environment to meet human needs, especially in the accelerated form we have experienced in recent centuries, has arguably tempted us to imagine that we are masters of the world and the authors of our own destiny. It has seduced us into forgetting, as Vaclav Havel famously put it, that we are not God.[3]

We are persuaded by our culture that we can have fulfillment without submission to authority. And, unwittingly, we take this formation

IN THE WORLDVIEW OF THE SEEKER, GOD IS STATIONARY, WAITING TO BE FOUND.

into the practice of our faiths. Our Gnostic context reconfigures our Christian discipleship. The religious sociologist Robert Wuthnow, in his book *After Heaven*,[4] noted that older forms of belief based on submission to a divine authority and religious duty—which he labeled religious "Dwelling"—had been replaced by new forms of faith, which emphasized greater individual autonomy and rejected traditional forms of religious authority and structure, which he called "Spiritual Seeking."

With our contemporary Gnostic sensibilities, we prefer to be the free-sounding spiritual seeker, rather than the tied-down religious dweller. Yet the word seeker is revealing. The Gnostic seeker must find God, to move through life seeking Him out. In the worldview of the seeker, the authority, the responsibility, the centrality is on the seeker. In this vision, God is stationary, waiting to be found. God is not really at the center of the drama; rather He is the supporting actor to the main player—the seeker.

However, in the biblical story, humans are not seekers; they are the sought. As Cyril O'Regan observes, the narrative of Gnosticism "represents a disfiguration . . . of the biblical narrative."[5] Gnosticism is an inverted gospel. In the true gospel, Jesus' sacrificial death upon the cross is the center of the drama. Grace is an unmerited gift, and we are secondary to the main player—God. Francis Thompson captured this truth in his poem "The Hound of Heaven," in which he feels the divine breath on the back of his neck as he flees from God through the alleyways of London, until God catches him and he collapses into submission and is washed with grace. We must dwell in grace under the one good and true King, Christ Jesus.

THE IMPLICIT AND THE EXPLICIT PROSPERITY GOSPEL

God-given limitations—the idea of being slaves for Christ—grates not only with the third culture but with elements of our Gnostic-influenced Christianity. Most of us recoil from the prosperity gospel that we encounter from strange televangelists on strange cable channels with even stranger hair, who tell us to send in our money now so that God will bless us with money and material possessions. We hear the stories of private jets and Rolls-Royces and rightly recoil in horror. Yet as much as we may scoff at this crass prosperity gospel, the mating of our faith with Gnosticism can create a more sophisticated implicit prosperity gospel. In this implicit prosperity gospel, if we do the right things, volunteer, turn up for church, contribute to that justice project, we can have the good life we see all around us in the West.

The prosperity gospel is garishly hawked by televangelists, whereas we subtly imbibe the implicit prosperity gospel through consumerism and advertising, but also through viewing the lives of other Christians who seem to lead amazing, meaningful, pleasure-filled lives. In a church that has pursued the strategy of cultural relevance, we only have to trawl through our Instagram feeds to find pastors, believing musicians, artists, authors, and activists who seem to live incredible lives. These people seem to have the best of both worlds: they follow Jesus and get to travel, live in cool neighborhoods, hang with really interesting people, have incredible marriages or rock the single life, and connect with the most amazing people. The more we view this, the more a belief inside of us rises.

> WE DO NOT RECOGNIZE THE WAY IN WHICH THE IMPLICIT PROSPERITY GOSPEL AFFECTS US UNTIL OUR UNSPOKEN EXPECTATIONS ARE NOT MET.

The belief is that if we do the stuff of Christianity—read our Bibles, help the poor, worship passionately, move the sound equipment without groaning—we will get a slice of the awesome Christian life that the implicit gospel promises. The strategy of cultural relevance will deliver for us too. If, in the explicit prosperity gospel, it is unthinkable that God would withhold from His faithful followers cash, cars, and mansions, in the implicit prosperity gospel of many, shaped by a culture that must elevate sex beyond its station in God's created order, we cannot imagine that God would ask of some celibacy. We do not recognize the way in which the implicit prosperity gospel affects us until our unspoken expectations are not met. Then the true extent of our belief is revealed. We understand that God would ask people in the Two-Thirds World to give up things—to sacrifice—but our heresy hidden under the surface is our belief that God would not ask Western people to deny themselves. Our alternative gospel is that we are Gnostic Christian seekers, searching for the good life, wanting the solace of faith with the autonomy of the third culture.

The radical descriptor that Scripture uses to describe the followers of Jesus is not seekers, but slaves. In 2 Corinthians 2:14 (ESV), Paul writes, "Thanks be to God, who in Christ always leads us in triumphal procession and through us spreads the fragrance of the knowledge of him everywhere." In 1 Corinthians 4:9 (NIV) Paul again uses this imagery to describe Christian discipleship, writing, "God has put us apostles on display at the end of the procession, like those condemned to die in the arena. We have been made a spectacle to the whole universe, to angels as well as to human beings."

When we read Paul's description of a triumphal procession, we most likely picture the championship team enjoying a ticker-tape parade or soldiers being cheered as they return home from overseas duty. Paul's readers in the Roman world would have had a very different mental image in their minds as they read this letter. With our usual understanding, the passage appears to endorse the kind of seeker-driven Christianity in which God leads us into the cultural good life. However, readers in Paul's time, familiar with the patterns of the Roman world, would have entertained a very different image.

A Triumphal Procession was an act of imperialistic propaganda. When a general or a Caesar had triumphed over a foreign people, they would pillage their cultural treasures and enslave their people, bringing them back to Rome in a parade of victory. At the head of the parade, the general or Caesar would stand in a chariot, covered in royal purple to be feted by the crowd, hailing him as the king of the people they had just defeated. Trailing behind in chains would be the former rulers, generals, and citizens of the vanquished country. Often upon reaching the end of the parade, a representative of the defeated people would be executed as an offering to the gods. The triumphal parade reinforced the power and violence of the Roman political system and the belief that a human can gain godlike autonomy and power.

In Jesus' death upon the cross we see an inverted triumphal procession. Jesus is paraded by Roman soldiers and given a crown and a purple royal robe. However, this is a crown of disgrace, a robe of mockery. He too is paraded through the streets, feted in sarcastic terms. The placard above His cross was a cynical ridiculing of His kingship. The soldiers mock, the crowd mocks, even the criminals on nearby crosses mock. Jesus hangs dying, humiliated, scorned, and powerless. Just as at the Roman Triumph a representative of the vanquished people is offered as a human sacrifice, Jesus dies an atoning death for the sins of humankind. It is a Roman centurion who finally understands, who, as he would hail a Caesar, recognizes a different kind of King, glorifying God. This is the upside-down kingdom. This is the inverted, subversive, triumphal procession. The believer in Christ is not a seeker, breaking past boundaries, transgressing limits, pursuing autonomy. They are transformed by grace, walking behind Christ in His triumphal procession as slaves to Christ. This selfless path of life, which gives up autonomy in order to find life in Christ, is incomprehensible to the third culture, as it has been to every culture of history. As Paul writes:

If our gospel is veiled, it is veiled to those who are perishing. In their
case, the god of this age has blinded the minds of the unbelievers so they
cannot see the light of the gospel of the glory of Christ, who is the image
of God. For we are not proclaiming ourselves but Jesus Christ as Lord,
and ourselves as your slaves because of Jesus. (2 Corinthians 4:3–4)

We are not seekers. We are slaves. The churches that do not fade and disappear in the third culture of the West will be churches that preach, teach, and live out the truth that we are called to live as slaves of Christ, a church fragrance of selflessness in a culture of selfishness. We are people who give up our autonomy not to unjust rulers or authorities, but to the one true King, the one good King, the King who has taken all of our rebellion, our sin, our injustice upon Himself. We lay our authority and autonomy down at the feet of the King with scars. The cross is the linchpin of the world: remove it and everything drifts apart. The Gnostic rebellion attempts a coup in the heavenly court. The job of creative minorities in the third culture is to live out the reality that the King has returned.

HEDONISM AND GRACE REVISITED

Evelyn Waugh's classic novel *Brideshead Revisited* tells the story of a family being torn apart by a search for pleasure. Told through the eyes of an atheistic young man, Charles Ryder, the work illustrates the lives of an aristocratic English family, the Marchmains, who are running from God. Charles's friend Sebastian Marchmain throws himself into a life of hedonism, eventually becoming a full-blown alcoholic, penniless and destitute in North Africa. Julia Marchmain, Sebastian's sister, begins an adulterous affair with Charles, which destroys her marriage. The patriarch of the family, Lord Marchmain, has for years lived with his Italian mistress in Venice, refusing to ever return to the faith of his youth. Waugh wrote that his novel "deals with what is theologically termed 'the operation of Grace,' that is to say, the unmerited and unilateral act of love by which God continually calls souls to Himself."[6]

Each of the characters seeks autonomy and knowingly breaks the commandments of their faith. Each attempts to cover their pain with the search for pleasure. Each runs as far from God as possible, only to find Him there. Sebastian discovers grace as, broken and alcoholic, he is taken in by kindly monks in Tunisia. Lord Marchmain, fighting with all his might to resist God, finally returns to his faith in his final moments. Julia, inspired by her father's deathbed conversion, breaks off her affair with Charles. Each in their own way finds their search for pleasure and autonomy apart from God, leading to the end of themselves, and there they find God's unmerited gift of loving grace.

G. K. Chesterton once observed that every man who knocked on the door of a brothel is searching for God. For in the second culture, there were always those who ran from God, seeking pleasure, who, like John Newton, lived the life of excess and sin, but who, coming to the end of themselves, could write, "Amazing Grace, how sweet the sound, that saved a wretch like me!" Yet in the third culture, the pursuit of pleasure takes on a Gnostic hue. In the second culture, Evelyn Waugh's Sebastian Marchmain, broken and at the end of himself, finds grace in a North African monastery. In the third culture tale of *SAFE*, Carol, isolated and at the end of herself, does not find grace, but can only vainly dig deeper into the self to find love. The Gnostic language of seeking and self-discovery seems to promise a life of pleasure and happiness, but in reality, it imprisons us.

HOW GNOSTICISM DESTROYS OUR SEARCH FOR PLEASURE AND UNDERMINES GRACE

Despite the West's obsession with sexual freedom and instant gratification, the third culture has not deteriorated into an orgiastic free-for-all that leads to society-wide collapse. Philosopher Gilles Lipovetsky notes that the contemporary individual thinks he is a pleasure seeker, but in reality his search for pleasure is stymied by a competitive society of high performance: "No longer can you voluptuously let yourself go. . . . What is being established is a culture of hyperactive performance without concrete or sensory reality—one which destroys the aims of the hedonistic lifestyle."[7] Instead of throwing themselves into a crazed life of sexual abandon with a string of partners, Dad sneaks a look at porn on his phone in the den, while upstairs his wife loses herself in *Fifty Shades of Grey* on her Kindle, before they both make it an early night to get the kids to football training in the morning. A young man, after taking Ecstasy two nights before, orders a breakfast consisting of a kale and ginger health shake because he is still preparing for the mini-marathon at the end of the month.

Of course, there are still those who come to the end of themselves through drink, drugs, sex, or gambling. At best, they are pitied; at worst, mocked and seen as weak creatures who could not hold together the quest for pleasure alongside pleasure. For the neo-Gnostic must always progress and improve. Our desire for earthly happiness and pleasure is tempered by our

> WHAT OUGHT TO BE WORRYING US THE MOST IS THE WAY IN WHICH PEOPLE'S PERSONALITIES HAVE BECOME MORE FRAGILE.

Gnostic push to refashion our lives and the world through efficiency. Therefore our culture, according to Lipovetsky, "tends to the disincarnation of pleasures."[8] Pleasure is pushed into the inner fantasy world and into online realms. Pleasures then have become desensualized, pushed away from concrete action into a realm of perpetual sinful possibility. This is something different; this is a halfhearted hedonism, a hovering sin of the mind, which promises to protect its indulger from the palpable sting of consequence. The beaten path to the door of the church is heavy with libertine footprints; however, this floating manifestation of sin presents a much greater challenge, both for the church and the sinner.

"What ought to be worrying us the most is not the way pleasure has become desensualized or turned into a 'dictatorship,' but the way in which people's personalities have become more fragile," Lipovetsky warns, noting that accompanying our increasing autonomy and freedom is a greater personal fragility. Lipovetsky continues,

> Hence the individual appears more and more opened up and mobile, fluid and socially independent. But this volatility signifies much more a destabilization of the self than a triumphant affirmation of a subject endowed with self-mastery—witness the rising tide of psychosomatic symptoms and obsessive-compulsive behavior, depression, anxiety and suicide attempts, not to mention the growing sense of inadequacy and self-deprecation. ... The more socially mobile the individual is, the more we witness signs of exhaustion and subjective "breakdowns"; the more freely and intensely people wish to live, the more we hear them saying how difficult life can be.[9]

As culture moves away from God, as the Gnostic self-shuns mediating institutions and collective norms, our culture becomes what sociologist Ulrich Beck labels as The Risk Society,[10] and Frank Furedi The Culture of Fear.[11] The individual, shorn of collective responsibility, traditional moral guidance, and binding relationships, finds that their freedom consists of negotiating a social and personal minefield of risk. Lipovetsky discerns that this fragility of the individual, and the demise of institutions, conventions, and traditions, leads us to buffer this anxiety and fragility by surrounding ourselves with pleasing spaces and enjoyable experiences. "We increasingly see hyper-individualistic passions for 'comfort and pleasure' and existential comfort, the demand for agreeable sensations, for a high-quality ambience and environment."[12] Thus we create a beautiful public world whose aesthetically pleasing design attempts to calm floundering Gnostics, as our anxiety provides a constant soundtrack to our inner world.

Chapter 7

Stop Catering to "Public" Opinion

HOW GNOSTICISM SUBSTITUTES REALITY FOR A DREAM WORLD

In comparison to so many other cinematic grimy, urban, and dystopian visions of the City of Angels, the sun-drenched, beautiful Los Angeles of Spike Jonze's 2013 film *Her* seems a utopia. Yet *Her* is in its own way an apocalyptic film. It contains an apocalypse you could almost miss. *Her's* protagonist Theodore Twombley (Joaquin Phoenix) falls in love with a computer program running on his phone, an operating system named Samantha powered by artificial intelligence and given voice by Scarlett Johansson. Samantha becomes at first an indispensable part of Theodore's life, then his primary companion, then his sexual partner. This relationship causes Theodore's life to collapse. Suffering breaks into Theodore's world. Theodore turns to Samantha because his own real-life marriage has failed, and he is unable to process his ex-wife's or his own emotions. Instead, he chooses the safety of a relationship with the non-human Samantha.

Theodore is a contemporary Gnostic. He is disengaged from the world, whilst at the same time being affable, earnest, and sensitive, much like the other citizens of *Her*'s Los Angeles. This air of disengagement has contributed to the breakdown of his marriage. His inner world is filled with the electronic fantasies of computer games, phone sex with strangers, and a disembodied sexual relationship with his operating system.

At one point in the film, Theodore is set up on a blind date with a beautiful woman. Theodore is obviously attracted to this woman, and the woman is smitten with Theodore, struggling to keep her hands off him. However, the moment that the woman asks if their attraction can move forward into a committed relationship, Theodore retreats, emotionally wounding the woman. Theodore's Gnostic sensibilities prefer to keep his autonomy intact rather than to enjoy the physical, embodied sexual pleasure that a committed relationship with the woman would bring. Theodore is sincere; he wants to be good, yet he can only operate from the Gnostic script he has been taught. He wishes for connection and companionship yet desires maximum freedom. The search for pleasure remains there but hovers in a Gnostic form, insulating him against the possibilities of consequence and responsibility.

Theodore, like so many today, drifts further from reality, drifting deeper into fantasy. As historian Michael Burleigh writes, Gnosticism ensures the "substitution of a dream world for reality."[1]

Near the end of the film, as Theodore walks through the city streets, in the crowd behind him no one is speaking; everyone stares intently at their phone; human interaction has disappeared, and the public square has died. A fiery comet has not dropped from the sky, nor has a terrorist mastermind set off a dirty bomb, nor has Godzilla descended upon the city in vengeance, yet an apocalypse of sorts has occurred. No one can see it because the city still stands, the lights blink, and the buildings, like the people, are still beautiful. Structurally the culture stands, yet emotionally, socially, and spiritually, it is disappearing. It is a kind of beautiful apocalypse. In the same way our third culture is a beautiful apocalypse. Everything falls apart while looking beautiful.

In the final scene of the movie, Theodore and his friend and fellow technological addict Amy sit atop a building. They are in silence, personally defeated. Around them the city stands untouched, everything is still stylishly designed and functioning. Theodore and Amy have become ghosts, people only half there, haunting a beautiful world. It is a complete reversal of the typical ending of an apocalyptic movie, in which the city is a heap of rubble, yet our protagonists have found in the midst of destruction a kind of inner fortitude. The destruction of their world has shown them what meaning really is. "The common faith is in the new life that succeeds human or global obliteration,"[2] writes cultural critic Marina Benjamin, noting that in the apocalyptic movie genre, destruction acts as a kind of purging, ridding greedy humans of their excess, giving them a chance to start again. Thus, while the city may be destroyed, the human spirit lives on stronger. In the beautiful apocalypse of *Her*, everything gets more beautiful while people internally fall apart.

Our sincerity, our desire for something greater, is stymied by our ironic beautiful world. This is not a functioning world, there is no sacred order; there is no home, no community, no institution, no church, no place where we can be loved unconditionally. It is simply a beautiful, designed, public space in which individuals seek autonomy and freedom, only to become paralyzed and anxious.

The culture of *Her* aligns with the cultural vision of the American philosopher Richard Rorty. Rorty proposed a kind of softer postmodern vision than many of his European counterparts. Rorty felt that many philosophers, in particular the Europeans, got too worked up over the fact that there was no meaning in the world. Instead of mourning the loss of meaning and heroically staring down nothingness, Rorty advocated, in the words of Peter Augustine Lawler, an "easygoing, sentimental, 'nice' culture."[3] Instead of religion, instead of philosophy, instead of trying to work it all out, Rorty advocates pragmatism, that we should simply accept our mortality and go about the business of creating a pleasant life for ourselves.

This was what Allan Bloom called "Nihilism without the abyss."[4] The late Richard John Neuhaus wrote that Rorty's secularist thought essentially stated, "Make it up as you go along; take ironic delight in the truth that there is no truth; there is no home that answers to our homelessness; definitely (but light-heartedly!) throw the final vocabulary that is your life in the face of nothingness. And if your neighbor or some inner curiosity persists in asking about the meaning of it all, simply change the subject."[5]

Both Richard John Neuhaus and Christopher Shannon point out Richard Rorty's vision of an ordered, beautiful, and hopeful public world held alongside a private realm of disordered, nihilistic self-creation. Shannon describes Rorty's vision as a "schizophrenic consensus," which "would have people shuttle back and forth between a practical quest for certainty in their 'public,' social lives, and an equally practical rejection of all certainty in their 'private,' individual lives."[6] Instead of a fully formed system of stories and spheres that informs the individual, the communal, the global, and the cosmic, our culture is divided into two spheres.

THE PUBLIC SPHERE

There is the public sphere—the societies of developed Western countries—that is stable and certain. The public sphere is a governed and pragmatic place with clear rules and expectations of how you are to behave. It is a world that is advancing, growing in comfort and wealth. It is not ostentatious but is defined by a clear aesthetic of tasteful beauty. The hopes of modernity are still here, technology still promises to make the world a better place, and politicians still attempt to promise peace and prosperity. This is the world you experience as you travel in the comfort of your car through well-signed and safe streets, past beautifully designed buildings, all while your phone guides you to your destination while simultaneously playing your favorite tunes. The coffee gets better, the food gets better, the design and the aesthetics get better. This is the world of things, buildings, travel, and matter. Everything is clearly defined, and there are no surprises, only the promise of a free, tolerant world and a hopeful future. Or at least that is what government and big business promise.

In the United States, more alert to the dangers found in the public space, the beautiful world is not so much found in downtowns as it is in the rest of the West. Instead Americans seek out reduced and secure spaces in the controlled environment of malls, reassuring restaurants, calming coffee shops, well-designed stores, cocooning homes, and the digitally gated communities of cyberspace.

CREATING A NICE LIFE

Either way, the idea of the "nice life" has taken powerful hold in the West (and, increasingly, other places as well). Philosopher Rorty believed that the best context to go about the business of creating a nice life is in a peaceful, materially prosperous, Western-style liberal democracy. Rorty, according to cultural historian Christopher Shannon, promoted a social vision based on "maximum material prosperity for all combined with an 'aestheticized culture' of self-creating individuals."[7] That is a vision of culture in which the public sphere continues to improve, becoming more beautiful, more liberal, more democratic, allowing the radical individual to pursue their desires to the fullest. For Rorty, as a philosopher who rejected the religious, the beautiful culture of the West approaches a kind of heaven on earth:

> *My sense of the holy, insofar as I have one, is bound up with the hope*
> *that someday, any millennium now, my remote descendants will live*
> *in a global civilization in which love is pretty much the only law. In*
> *such a society, communication would be domination-free, class and*
> *caste would be unknown, hierarchy would be a matter of temporary*
> *pragmatic convenience, and power would be entirely at the disposal*
> *of the free agreement of a literate and well-educated electorate. I have*
> *no idea how such a society could come about. It is, one might say, a*
> *mystery. This mystery, like that of the Incarnation, concerns the coming*
> *into existence of a love that is kind, patient, and endures all things.*[8]

This is a culture in which we believe that ultimately, life is meaningless, but we are insulated from the full horror of such a belief by the distracting and anesthetizing qualities of our public culture. Our existential angst is drowned out by cooking shows, discount airfares, smartphones, and celebrity gossip. But what of those who still cling to desires for something more, a yearning for a transcendent belief, centered on more than just a tolerant society?

Rorty does not advocate that those who believe should be expunged from society altogether, rather such people need to keep their spiritual and metaphysical longings to themselves, or be joshed out of their beliefs. See them as nuts, roll your eyes at them, and if they continue in their belief, walk away. Let government, education, and corporations, led by educated, nice, sophisticated individuals, reeducate them or at least their children into the "easygoing atheism" of the beautiful world. The hope of our culture is that dissenting believers will eventually be reeducated as all minorities and distinctions dissolve into a sea of Western, materialist sophisticates. The beautiful, public sphere of our culture is the architecture of our disbelief. It soothes us, gives us vain hope, and distracts us, all while our private world becomes more fragile.

THE PRIVATE SPHERE

Under the clearly defined space of the public world, there is the private realm. This is a very different world. Here, there are no clear rules; there is no definition. There is little if any meaning to be sought outside of the individual. In fact, meanings, rules, and received traditions must be deconstructed, submitted to the ultimate judgment of the individual who has no authoritative basis to judge their worth beyond their own opinions. With faith, higher beliefs, and grand visions expelled from the public world, it is left to the individual to follow the Gnostic project, to create their own belief system and generate their own meaning, to craft, shape, and discover their identities.

> WE ARE CALLED TO LIVE OUT AND PREACH THE GOSPEL IN AN AGE THAT CARESSES US AS IT CORRODES OUR FAITH AND TRUST IN JESUS.

Even love is remodeled in this vision of a beautiful, comfortable culture. The self-denying love so valued throughout history is questioned. Romantic love, with its desire for erotic, transcendent union, is reduced into what Rorty calls "casual, friendly copulation"—the kind of reduced, physical couplings we see in today's Tinder sexual landscape in which sex becomes mechanical. Devoid of responsibility and relationship, sex becomes an exercise in accounting, a racking up of numbers.

In such an environment friendship is also diminished. Media theorist Jaron Lanier notes that when we "have accumulated thousands of friends on Facebook . . . this can only be true if the idea of friendship is reduced."[9] This depersonalized vision is the dream of a small utopia, a beautiful world made for the individual to pursue their dreams of freedom and self-creation. The stability and protection that committed, covenantal relationships bring is undermined by the third culture; and the self, in pursuit of unlimited freedom, becomes more unstable.

```
┌─────────────────────────────────────────────────────────┐
│                         PUBLIC                          │
│                                                         │
│                                                         │
└─────────────────────────────────────────────────────────┘
```

```
┌─────────────────────────────────────────────────────────┐
│                         PRIVATE                         │
│                                                         │
│                                                         │
└─────────────────────────────────────────────────────────┘
```

This private realm is unstable, and constantly changing. Each decision must be questioned alongside countless other opportunities. The beautiful world and its endless choices must be negotiated, and commitments are eroded, seen as impediments to the possibility of happiness and fulfillment. Whereas once culture attempted to either ennoble its citizens or maintain the status quo, now our culture exists to seduce us. Zygmunt Bauman observes:

> Our culture today consists of offers, not prohibitions; propositions, not norms. . . . Culture today is engaged in laying down temptations and setting up attractions, with luring and seducing, not with normative regulation; with PR rather than police supervision; with the production, sowing and planting of new needs and desires, rather than with duty. . . . Its chief concern is to prevent a feeling of satisfaction . . . and in particular to counteract their perfect, complete and definitive gratification, which would leave no room for further, new and as yet unfulfilled needs and whims.[10]

The beautiful world pitches to the believer a constant and never-ending array of options, temptations, and tantalizing choices. Not only must the Christian face the pressure of an increasingly hostile secular culture, but that culture offers us a cornucopia of bounty, while undermining the legitimacy and functionality of Christian commitment in our hearts and minds. Whereas in the past the believer sometimes faced doubt, now the contemporary believer faces a barrage of doubt, not just over their faith, but their choices and their commitments. We are called to live out and preach the gospel in an age that caresses us as it corrodes our faith and trust in Jesus.

THE CHURCH AND THE PUBLIC/PRIVATE SPLIT

If the church acted as the public sphere, it could grow, be hopeful, and attract a crowd. It could gain influence and seeming success, and be loved by its people—while in the private sphere, its members and attenders would remain a confused mess of commitment-phobia, compartmentalization, and self-creation. If Richard Rorty's vision of an "ironically delightful" society exists, one that offers its citizens a public sphere of comfort, beauty, order, and hope in which to pursue their own nihilistic dreams of self-creation, we have to ask: Did the church operate as a similar public sphere? An ordered, comfortable, and beautiful space, a tool for self-creation to be accessed when so desired, and then to be abandoned when no longer needed? Such a situation could only occur when an extraordinary gap had grown between our private and public spheres, when two divergent world-views could operate in both.

This could only occur when the public sphere ultimately was sub-servient to the wishes, wants, and desires of the individual. In such an environment, people had grown ghostly because they were only half there; the script of culture had taught them to view public spheres as spaces in which to self-create. As Thomas Bergler warns, "Even if they like church, such Christians are tempted to see it as a tool for personal fulfillment."[11] The church was never called to help individuals self-create.

BEING TRANSFORMED BY THE RENEWING OF OUR MINDS

There are some parallels between our culture with its split between public and private spheres and the Roman world in which the early church grew and flourished. The Roman culture offered public space, roads, forums, aqueducts, and law and order, and it also offered a civil religion. Yet the Roman citizen in their private world faced a dizzying choice of cults, mystery religions, and schools of philosophy all competing for attention and commitment. We can understand when Tom Wright makes the claim that "Gnosticism flourishes in a world of empire. Each sustains the other. The empire encourages Gnosticism by creating a world where, for most people, there seems no possibility of escape from its all-conquering power, and by encouraging types of religion which offer an otherworldly escape, and therefore see no need to offer a critique of empire, still less an alternative to it. Nothing's going to change: escape into a private spirituality! Gnosticism then at least tacitly encourages empire, by leading its devotees into that escapist spirituality, leaving the kingdoms of the world to be divided up by others."[12]

In our contemporary secular Gnostic culture, our private escape is not into the esoteric spiritual mysteries of the cults, but it is otherworldly. Our private lives, like Theodore Twombley's, are damaged by the retreat into fantasies fueled by consumerism, the age of the image, the disengagement of social media, and the varieties of disembodied sexual experiences on offer. Unlike the Gnosticism of the ancient world, our Gnostic escape still draws us into the self and the world; our fantasies are still focused on this world.

IN THE WORLD BUT NOT OF IT?

Those shaped by the gospel understand that they are in the world but not of it. As we have learned, the beautiful world that surrounds us undermines our faith by providing constant temptations and seductions, offering us contentment, a kind of achievable heaven on earth. A consumer order as exists in our world is powered by our constant dissatisfaction. To foster a sense of dissatisfaction, the world must offer us everything, and the beautiful world does indeed seem to promise such a feat. This reality is made even more toxic for our faith in combination with a belief that has taken hold in the Christian world: that we are too heavenly minded to do any earthly good.

Our fixation with relevance can lead us to believe that we, or the Christian culture as a whole, are too concerned with spiritual fairy floss than earthly kingdom realities. As J. K. A. Smith notes, "Many evangelicals are reacting to the dualism of their fundamental heritage that seemed to only value 'heaven' and offered no functional affirmation of the importance of 'this life.' Their rejection of this finds expression in a new emphasis on 'the goodness of creation' and the importance of social justice."[13] Across the spectrum of Christian belief, we see this shift from new-Reformed evangelicals who wish to influence the spheres of culture, to charismatic churches offering seminars on parenting and finances, to social justice movements making change in the world, to earthy missional churches in pubs, to the professional presentation panache of Pentecostal churches. Smith is not saying these things are wrong in and of themselves. He is warning us of the cultural force of secularism that reduces our focus to the immanent.

In the beautiful world, there is a point in which many realize that while their hip and fantastic church may offer them opportunities to engage in justice projects, a life group that meets for community and meal at the pub, and digestible life advice, they can leave the church and find similar opportunities. The kicker is that you can still enjoy all of this while ditching the biblical prohibitions on sex, or having to measure up to the limitations of biblical holiness, or the commitments of creedal Christian community. If you still want to keep your

PARADOXICALLY, ONLY OTHERWORLDLINESS GUARANTEES PROPER ENGAGEMENT IN THIS WORLD.

sneaker toe in the Christian camp, no problem. Just pick up a book or subscribe to that podcast by a "progressive" Christian author who will reassure you that you can still be a Christian while not getting too stressed about sex or Scripture or going to church.

In an increasingly world-focused evangelical church, what looks like leaving faith or church, to the actual leaver simply seems like a small shimmy to the left, in which the beautiful world promises that you can have it all.

"HEAVENLY PARTICIPATION"

To be sure, there were periods in Christian history when believers were too focused upon heaven and neglected this world. However, this increasing shift away from heaven in the Western church was detected by C. S. Lewis as early as the 1940s when he remarked,

> If you read history you will find that the Christians who did most for the present world were just those who thought most of the next. The Apostles themselves, who set on foot the conversion of the Roman Empire, the great men who built up the Middle Ages, the English Evangelicals who abolished the Slave Trade, all left their mark on Earth, precisely because their minds were occupied with Heaven. It is since Christians have largely ceased to think of the other world that they have become so ineffective in this. Aim at Heaven and you will get earth "thrown in": aim at earth and you will get neither.[14]

Theologian Hans Boersma calls this kind of aiming at heaven and getting earth thrown in "heavenly participation," noting that in the writings of Paul, "It is not as though believers here on earth somehow identify with a faraway place called 'heaven.' Rather, they have a real or participatory connection with heaven. . . . Participation in heaven changes life on earth: paradoxically, only otherworldliness guarantees proper engagement in this world." In this engagement, "not only is heaven the 'place' in which Christians are already at home today, but it also marks their origin and aim."[15]

This point is key: we live in the world and are called to flourish within it, yet we must always remember that the end point of that flourishing is heaven. Some things of this world will seem to promise flourishing, but in the end will produce corruption. The good things of this world must be understood as pointing toward heaven and the creator of all good things. Lewis offers this helpful definition:

> *Most of us find it very difficult to want "Heaven" at all—except in so far as "Heaven" means meeting again our friends who have died. One reason for this difficulty is that we have not been trained: our whole education tends to fix our minds on this world. Another reason is that when the real want for Heaven is present in us, we do not recognize it. Most people, if they had really learned to look into their own hearts, would know that they do want, and want acutely, something that cannot be had in this world. There are all sorts of things in this world that offer to give it to you, but they [don't] quite keep to their promise. The longings which arise in us when we first fall in love, or first think of some foreign country, or first take up some subject that excites us, are longings which no marriage, no travel, no learnings, can really satisfy. I am now not speaking of what would be ordinarily called unsuccessful marriages, or holidays, or learned careers. I am speaking of the best possible ones. There was something we grasped at, in the first moment of longing, which just fades away in the reality.[16]*

The beautiful world seems to offer the potential to possess beautiful things and experiences. However, in possessing them we fail to acknowledge their role as gifts, given for our enjoyment with instructions on how to best enjoy them. A gift is ultimately a thing of grace. When we try to possess a gift, to claim it as our own, we rob it of its grace. We insult and ignore the giver of the gift. This was the sin of Adam. It was the sin of Israel as it attempted to possess the gifts of creation, even going as far as worshiping them. For eventually, as Israel tried to possess things, the things, the idols, possessed and owned them. Instead of stewarding the world, the world stewarded them. Isaiah writes,

> All who fashion idols are nothing, and the things they delight in do not profit. Their witnesses neither see nor know, that they may be put to shame. Who fashions a god or casts an idol that is profitable for nothing? Behold, all his companions shall be put to shame, and the craftsmen are only human. Let them all assemble, let them stand forth. They shall be terrified; they shall be put to shame together.

> The ironsmith takes a cutting tool and works it over the coals. He fashions it with hammers and works it with his strong arm. He becomes hungry, and his strength fails; he drinks no water and is faint. The carpenter stretches a line; he marks it out with a pencil. He shapes it with planes and marks it with a compass. He shapes it into the figure of a man, with the beauty of a man, to dwell in a house. He cuts down cedars, or he chooses a cypress tree or an oak and lets it grow strong among the trees of the forest. He plants a cedar and the rain nourishes it. Then it becomes fuel for a man. He takes a part of it and warms himself; he kindles a fire and bakes bread. Also he makes a god and worships it; he makes it an idol and falls down before it. Half of it he burns in the fire. Over the half he eats meat; he roasts it and is satisfied. Also he warms himself and says, "Aha, I am warm, I have seen the fire!" And the rest of it he makes into a god, his idol, and falls down to it and worships it. He prays to it and says, "Deliver me, for you are my god!"

> They know not, nor do they discern, for he has shut their eyes, so that they cannot see, and their hearts, so that they cannot understand. No

*one considers, nor is there knowledge or discernment to say, "Half of it
I burned in the fire; I also baked bread on its coals; I roasted meat and
have eaten. And shall I make the rest of it an abomination? Shall I fall
down before a block of wood?" He feeds on ashes; a deluded heart has
led him astray, and he cannot deliver himself or say, "Is there not a lie
in my right hand?" (Isaiah 44:9–20 ESV)*

In the above passage, we see the entire sweep of human ingenuity,
the breadth of human creativity. We see humans attempting to live
out their vocation. They bake bread, shape steel, and sculpt wood into
beautiful forms. Minus the Spirit of God, such an endeavor ultimately
sees the creational order inverted. Instead of humans worshiping God
and flourishing as they cultivate and create out of the raw materials of
the earth, pointing everything back to God as an act of worship, we
see humans making gods out of the lowest forms of life. Things are
elevated to the place of God. Earth cannot replace God.

Without God, humans attempt to create a beautiful world, filled
with fine foods, craftsmanship, fulfilling work, elegant forms, and
creativity. Yet this beautiful world becomes a prison as humans are
possessed by the things that they create. We are unable to understand
or even see the world correctly as a gift from God, to be enjoyed, but
not owned. The contemporary Gnostic wishes to escape the actual
reality of the world, to hide from the mundane, from responsibility,
from suffering. The promises of our culture show us a public world
where this seems possible. George Weigel writes:

*The new Gnosticism is like a defective pair of glasses; we can't see
reality clearly through its warped lenses. So what is the antidote to
this Gnostic myopia and astigmatism? The answer is seeing the world
through biblical lenses, through lenses ground by the biblical depiction
of the human condition, which the people of the Church can come to
know by effective biblical preaching that, like the expository preaching*

> *of the Fathers of the Church, allows the people of the Church to see*
> *clearly—themselves, their neighbors, this historical moment, and this*
> *moment's place amid the in-breaking kingdom.*[17]

One of those church fathers, Irenaeus, who confronted the rise of Gnosticism in the early church, understood that Gnosticism disfigured our view of the world. Irenaeus's rebuttal to Gnosticism is a theology of grace, showing that sin and our quest to be gods tears us and the world apart. Humans and the world can only be made whole again through Christ and His cross. Of Irenaeus's response, von Balthasar reflects,

> *The thought of Irenaeus forms a great axis. Its first movement is steep*
> *and Godward. From the icy arrogance and worldly secrecies of Gnos-*
> *ticism, it flies straight to the saving heights of the ever-greater God,*
> *whom no mind can grasp. The other movement is broad, slow, heavy,*
> *a line drawn across the face of the earth. In contrast to the Gnostic's*
> *empty spiritualism . . . he stubbornly refuses to let man cut himself off*
> *from the life of this world and escape into a pseudo-heavenly half-exis-*
> *tence. . . . At the centre of this axis is the image of the Son of Man, who*
> *unites heaven and earth. He is the first touchstone of the Christian*
> *truth. Only in Him is there resolution of the paradox which Gnosticism*
> *tried in vain to master. God by nature is invisible, yet man by nature*
> *desires the vision of God. But this uniting of God and world take place*
> *in the Passion of Christ, when He is stretched out between height and*
> *depth, breadth and length. The cross-beams are the world's true center,*
> *and since it is in this sign that all creation is redeemed, they become the*
> *"watermark" of any kind of existence in the world.*[18]

Only the cross can hold together both the world and heaven. Only the cross can rejoin our public and private worlds. It shows us the way to properly live in and enjoy creation. We are not to escape, and we are not to possess; we are to sacrifice. The slaves of Christ understand that the world is God's. It is not to be possessed, rather it points back to Him. Alexander Schmemann writes,

> It is the movement that Adam failed to perform, and that in Christ has become the very life of man: a movement of adoration and praise in which all joy and suffering, all beauty and all frustration, all hunger and satisfaction are referred to their ultimate End and become finally meaningful. Yes, to be sure, it is a sacrifice: but sacrifice is the most natural act of man, the very essence of his life. Man is a sacrificial being, because he finds his life in love, and love is sacrificial: it puts the value, the very meaning of life in the other and gives life to the other, and in this giving, in this sacrifice, finds the meaning and joy of life. We offer the world and ourselves to God. But we do it in Christ and in remembrance of Him. We do it in Christ because He has already offered all that is to be offered to God.[19]

The believer is called to live sacrificially, offering back to God everything that is His, enjoying the gifts of this world yes, but offering them back to God, using them as an opportunity to worship the Creator of all good gifts. Our faith, our resilience in the face of the beautiful world, comes from the way that the cross enables us to hold both earth and heaven together. The horizontal axis of the cross points us toward the world, enabling us to enjoy creation in its right place, while the vertical axis points us back to the worship of the Creator of all things.

Resilient believers view creation and the world through the prism of the cross. This leads to the creative tension behind the life of faith—the familiar "in but not of" the world.

Chapter 8

Don't Offer Everything.
Deliver Truth.

AL-QAEDA IS DESTROYED BY THE THIRD CULTURE

In his last days, Osama bin Laden had a lot to be worried about. Drones constantly buzzed above the heads of his men, unleashing their fury out of the sky. Electronic surveillance by their enemies ensured that all communication now had to be laboriously passed on across the world by hand-delivered, written letters. Bin Laden worried about being poisoned, about climate change, and about the low morale of his organization. In the wake of the attacks of 9/11, Al-Qaeda was riding a high. Not only was it the premier terrorist organization in the world for jihadists, Western organizational experts hailed its fluid, swarm-like structure as the kind of networked future for organizations across the world. Yet a few years later, everything had changed.

One of the significant problems facing Al-Qaeda was the lack of discipline and commitment being shown by new recruits from wealthier, more developed countries. The ascendancy of the self, driven by the West, was having an effect upon the terrorist organization. The battle-hardened leadership of Al-Qaeda was tearing out their hair, trying to manage recruits who would turn up to training one day and not the next. Instead of planning attacks upon the West, Al-Qaeda members were having to waste time dragging recruits back from their shopping sprees at local markets, repeatedly telling them to stay off their phones. Recruits exhaustively trained and groomed for missions but would simply one day disappear like ghosts, having lost interest.

Al-Qaeda's much-lauded, networked, decentralized organizational structure was useless in dealing with this ghostlike commitment. "We have some other problems . . . like dissent and lack of discipline," wrote one of bin Laden's deputies in exasperation to his commander, complaining that these new recruits "do as they wish and roam in the markets. They are not associated with any group and they have no obedience. Sometimes, some of them participate in jihad, while others make no contribution to jihad. A solution to the problem they represent has escaped us, but we are still trying."[1] It's no wonder that in the last video of bin Laden released, we see him silently watching television in a dark room, draped in a blanket, a fragile, tired man leading a fragile, tired movement.

Al-Qaeda's leadership had coalesced in the tough battlefields of Afghanistan during the Soviet invasion. Bin Laden and his compatriots had sacrificed comfortable, wealthy lives to fight for a cause. This process instilled in them a military discipline and fortitude. It was this dedication that allowed its members to go undercover for years in Western cities, before unleashing martyr missions. Al-Qaeda's appeal was rooted in what journalist Moise's Naim labels Code; that is, an appeal to a higher, religious, or communal motivation, which would ensure commitment to the cause and leadership of the movement. Code, according to Naim, "does not employ coercion; instead it activates our sense of moral duty."[2] This activation of duty originates as "a higher and unquestioned power unequivocally tells us how to behave." Code had worked for Al-Qaeda, just as it had worked throughout human history for movements, be they noble, evil, or benign.

THE REVOLUTION AGAINST CODE

Al-Qaeda, like so many other organizations that rely on a moral code, faced the challenge of recruiting in an age where the individual increasingly finds a moral, binding call incomprehensible. Philip Rieff, in exploring the dynamics of the third culture of the West, observed a revolution against code and all commitments.[3]

In contrast to the dominant Western view of secularism, which sees a gradual evolution toward a progressive, enlightened culture, Rieff saw culture lurching between revolutions of release and revolutions of restraint. Any culture consists of a set of moral commands. These commands tell us what to do and what not to do. In any culture, these commands are under constant pressure from those within the society, so key figures within the culture act as moral authorities, communicating the rationale of the moral commands and exemplifying them with their personal lives. This is the influential power of code.

> THE SOLDIERS OF THE ISLAMIC STATE TOOK BATTLEFIELD SELFIES AND LIVE-TWEETED WHILE IN THE MIDST OF COMBAT.

When the moral commands come under too much pressure, eventually they are rejected and a revolution of release begins, led by those whose authority consists of undermining the moral commands and breaking them personally. The cultural mood shifts from obeying the moral commands to breaking them. Release replaces restraint as the dominant social mode. Code loses power to influence. Duty is rejected. The individual must discover the ways in which they had internalized the old moral commands and then break them. Any forms of external authority, self-denial, and morality must be expelled, for they have replaced sin as the new sin. Those who once guarded the moral commands are the new enemy to be demonized and defined against; in their place the maverick, the rebel, and the releaser are the new elite.

Rieff noted that groups who continue to operate from a moral code during a revolution of release are tarred with the brush of being controllers. In these eras, including our contemporary revolution of release, anyone who holds to external religious truths, who submits to moral commands and traditions, will be automatically tarred as controllers, repressive and oppressive.

ISIS, THE MUTANT CHILD OF THE THIRD CULTURE

In an interview with Britain's *Guardian* newspaper,[4] two senior leaders of Al-Qaeda complained that the emergence of the Islamic State had ripped their movement apart, and that it was no longer functional. The Islamic State was both a reaction against the third culture and also a mutant, anarchic child of it. Alongside local disaffected Sunni tribes, it recruited and inspired from the West young people who were both reacting against, and defined by, the third culture.

Al-Qaeda prohibited its members from using electronic communications and from using their phones. In contrast, the soldiers of the Islamic State took battlefield selfies and live-tweeted while in the midst of combat. They hashtagged Instagram photos with tags such as #Jihadlyfe, while flirting online with female Islamic State groupies, some of whom made their way from their homes in the West, without their parents' consent, to snag a hot, rebel jihadist. Al-Qaeda promotional videos usually consisted of the talking head of bin Laden or his associate and successor Ayman al-Zawahiri, lecturing and reading out statements. Videos produced by the Islamic State were lushly shot, promising alienated and directionless potential recruits a kind of real-life Game of Thrones or Call of Duty existence, in which they would find personal meaning and glory.

Videos and photos showed Islamic State fighters from the West, riding around captured towns in BMWs, extorting plunder from captured minorities. Whereas Al-Qaeda are always imagined hiding away in caves, the Islamic State's promotions promised the kind of infrastructure that would ensure the jihadist comfort and security. One promotional video featured a young, blue-eyed pediatrician with Australian-accented English showing the kind of postnatal care offered in the Islamic State. If you muted the sound, you could mistake the video for a health fund commercial. Other videos featured English-language schools for the children of foreign fighters. The message of the Islamic State essentially said that you can partake in armed jihad while having your personal dreams come true alongside Western levels of healthcare. Why wait for virgins and glory in the afterlife when you can have them now?

In a revolution of release, in which individual autonomy reigns supreme, "pitch" becomes one of the only modes of communication and coercion. If one wants to recruit others to a cause or movement, in the revolution of release you must promise benefits to the individual. This is where the Islamic State outmaneuvered Al-Qaeda in the competitive game of jihadist recruitment. Whereas Al-Qaeda demanded discipline and obedience, and recruited through code, the Islamic State in Naim's language used pitch—that is, the promise of tangible, attractive benefits—in order to cut through the messaging of the various jihadist groups. The religious, apocalyptic language of the Islamic State's recruiting at times sounds like code but underneath it clearly is pitch—the lure of personal benefit—promising potential recruits a life of glory and personal meaning within the caliphate.

CODE

Motivated by a
higher religious, or
communal duty.
Self-denying for a
higher cause.

PITCH

Motivated by the
promise of gratification
and reward. Self-
expanding through
personal benefit.

WHEN RELIGION PITCHES

Pitches that promise tangible benefits have overtaken codes and commands that appeal to discipline and commitment. As the cultural landscape becomes more crowded with competing agendas and claims for commitment, greater promises need to be made to cut through the buzz. In this new environment, one can gather a group or movement; you have tools available to you such as the Internet. The tricky bit is maintaining the commitment in the face of constant temptation. The average citizen lives in a world of continual promise and allurement. Both large organizations and the most fluid, decentralized networks find themselves weakened, as the basic ingredients of commitment, presence, attention, and sacrifice are corroded by the constant lure of something better.

It is worth noting that it is not just consumerism that pitches to us, but today the mode of pitch is used by governments, the military, NGOs, and, as Naim observes, religion:

Consider, for instance the power of religion, which operates through
multiple channels. Dogma or moral code, whether enshrined in age-old
scripture or propounded by a latter-day preacher or guru, is a big
part of what earns an organized faith its adherents—along with their
commitment of time and belief, their presence at services, their tithes,
and their labor. But when churches, temples, and mosques compete

for members, they often do so on the basis of a pitch, as in advertising.
Indeed, many institutions of faith stage elaborate campaigns managed
by highly specialized advertising firms. And they offer rewards as
well—not just immaterial reward of promised salvation but here-and-
now benefits.[5]

The great problem is that to compete with all the other pitches you have to improve your own, either implicitly or explicitly amplifying the tangible benefits on offer. While pitch can deliver you recruits or keep existing members within your organization, eventually a gap will appear between what you can pitch and what you can deliver. Part of the Islamic State's devilish genius is that it understands this. A movement based just on pitch and individual glory could not have produced the military commitment and discipline needed to capture the huge swaths of territory that it has won while under sustained attack on multiple fronts. ISIS's "pitch" disappears once a recruit hits the ground in Syria and Iraq.

Whereas Al-Qaeda has drafted climate change initiatives and pondered introducing their more wealthy members to poorer African jihadists to increase their commitment levels, ISIS will kill you if you decide to return home to Mom because life on the ground isn't like the videos. The Islamic State recruits with pitch and keeps you there with the threat of violence.

CREDIT CARD CHURCH

In the '80s, the social demographer Daniel Yankelovich studied the radical changes that were occurring in American culture as older forms of duty gave way to the new individualism.[6] Yankelovich observed that the unencumbered, hedonistic, norm-free lifestyle promoted by the new rules of individual autonomy had to be funded by a certain personal financial well-being. One had to have the money to afford things such as travel, entertainment, and adventure. One also had to find themselves in an employment situation which was light on responsibility and which allowed incredible flexibility to drop everything to follow one's desires.

Yankelovich pointed out that the irony was that one needed a certain baseline financial and employment security to generate the kind of free-form lifestyle that culture had set as the ideal, but that the free-form lifestyle ate up one's wealth and undermined their employment abilities. Yankelovich's research found that those who were pursuing the new lifestyle were primarily university-educated 18–35-year-olds who were able to pursue their lifestyle because they were doing so on the back of their parents' and grandparents' ethic of self-sacrifice. The self-fulfilling, norm-free life ethic lived parasitically off the self-sacrificing, norm-filled life ethic.

Such an approach, however, had limitations.

Debt, in particular credit cards, became one solution to this issue, gaining popularity as the new individualism became the norm. Individuals sacrificed their future financial well-being for present enjoyment and freedom. Many today who live exciting and pleasure-filled lives in their twenties and thirties will find their older years marked by poverty and struggle. In the same way, many churches are sacrificing the future for the immediate when they pitch. As organizations—and indeed churches—switch from a higher call for commitment and self-sacrifice to a pitch that promises tangible and immediate benefits, the results can initially seem successful. We can attract attendees and members, sometimes in large numbers.

> IN THE SECULAR WEST, WE ARE ADDICTED TO TRYING TO ASCERTAIN WHERE THE CULTURE CURRENTLY STANDS ON FAITH.

Yet eventually, when we just rely on pitch, we must run into the problem of disappearance, as loosely committed adherents hang around, and half-commitment thrives while waiting for the promise of the pitch to be realized. We gain the immediate benefit of reaching and attracting people, but if they have just come for the pitch, wanting spiritual succor and community, while maintaining and maximizing their own personal autonomy, eventually the debt must be paid by both the church and the individual believer. Attenders disappear when the pitch is not realized, or they move on to respond to another pitch given elsewhere. Many churches gain numbers and success in the short term, but in essence, they operate their ministries and churches on the vapors of the commitments of past generations. This is a strategy that can only last for so long.

Recruiting and building churches and movements around code is difficult. It requires face-to-face contact, it requires patience, and it is messy. We are drawn to pitch because often we find it easier to grasp the concept of the public and their view of faith, rather than imagining the complexity of individuals. Polls and demographics appear to give us graspable, measurable indicators of where people are at spiritually. In the secular West, we are addicted to trying to ascertain where the culture currently stands on faith. Like a nervous politician watching the polls, our self-esteem as the church can sometimes appear connected to the latest round of stats surveying faith. A drop of mere percentage points can send us into the doldrums.

PITCHING TO THE PUBLIC

In his book *This Present Age*, which warned and pointed toward the kind of disengaged culture in which we live today, Søren Kierkegaard warned of the danger of trying to win over the public. For the public was really "a phantom, its spirit, a monstrous abstraction, an all-embracing something, which is nothing, a mirage—and that phantom is the public. It is only in an age which is without passion, yet reflective, that such a phantom can develop itself with the help of the Press which itself becomes an abstraction. . . . There is no such thing as a public."[7]

Ultimately, the public is a Gnostic creation, a disembodied force that garners tremendous power. Jesus understood that crowds are ghostlike; they make luminous, frightening appearances, but disperse and disappear in a moment. They could not be trusted, and a ministry—let alone a kingdom—could not be built upon them. As Kierkegaard illuminates, in the modern age, the public is even more ghostlike. "Only when the sense of association in society is no longer strong enough to give life to concrete realities is the Press able to create that abstraction 'the public,' consisting of unreal individuals who never are and never can be united in an actual situation or organization and yet are held together as a whole."[8] The lack of social structures and the individualism of our age creates the need for the phantom of the public, observes Kierkegaard.

When we no longer know people well enough to gauge what is going on, the press and the media attempts to fill this relational gap by telling us what others think and reporting on public opinion. The public is this ghostly entity who is always present, who always has an opinion, and who, in the age of democracy, is always right. Yet they are also a phantom, they don't exist anywhere in concrete form, they cannot be challenge, they have no responsibility, and they commit no actions. They are simply the calculated guess of what some demographic professionals estimate the majority of people are thinking. Yet the phantom of the public carries so much power in the mind of today's Christian.

Eugene Peterson writes, "Crowds lie. The more people, the less truth. . . . In crowds the truth is flattened to fit a slogan. Not only the truth spoken, but the truth that is lived is reduced and distorted by the crowd. The crowd makes spectators of us, passive in the presence of excellence or beauty. The crowd makes consumers of us, inertly taking in whatever is pushed at us. As spectators and consumers the central and foundational elements of our being human—our ability to create, our drive to excel, our capacity to commune with God—atrophy."[9]

We obsess over the percentage of Christians in our nation or city, and we fret and chatter as public opinion is revealed in percentage form over complex social and theological issues. We wish the press would give faith a more even-handed approach, and we are driven to change public opinion. Part of us wishes we could be thrown off a high building in the public square and plucked out of the sky by angels, in order to dazzle the phantom public. Yet a positive public opinion will not establish the kingdom of God. We do well to heed the advice of Kierkegaard that "a public is a phantom which forbids all personal contact. And if a man adopts public opinion today and is hissed to-morrow he is hissed by the public."[10]

> JESUS UNDERSTOOD THAT CROWDS COULD NOT BE TRUSTED.

Instead what is real are individuals, communities, families, groups, and neighborhoods, people you can eat with, talk to, and listen to. These are not demographic phantoms, but real people. If you were to have taken a poll of Christian belief in Israel at about 6 a.m. Jerusalem time on the morning of Pentecost, the results would have shown that the gospel had lost in the court of public opinion; you could have fit the paltry responders in the positive into a small-ish room. But that is precisely the point; rather than public opinion, a small, living, breathing, devoted, Spirit-filled bunch of actual human beings was what Jesus was building His kingdom upon.

We need to release ourselves from the addiction of trying to win over the public and the burden of trying to influence public opinion, of trying to build ministries upon pitch alone. Instead we need to remember that if we are to build resilient disciples in our "on-to-the-next-shiny-thing" culture, we need to do as Jesus did and focus on the concreteness of actual people. We see Jesus building His ministry upon going deep with a few, rather than going shallow with the public.

I am not making an argument either against large churches or for smaller churches; the practice of going deep with the few can be adhered to in any environment. In contrast to the shifting, swirling ephemerality of public opinion, Kierkegaard advocates that individuals be formed and shaped directly, "taught to be content, in the highest religious sense, with himself and his relationship with God, to be at one with himself instead of being in agreement with a public which destroys everything that is relative, concrete and particular in life; educated to find peace within himself and with God, instead of counting hands."[11]

Contentment is at the heart of our fixation on the court of public opinion.[12] We wish to understand what the public thinks because the public is the seemingly most visible manifestation of what the world thinks. It is a kind of alternate revelation to the Word of God. If public opinion shifts into our favor, then the discomfort we feel and the lack of belonging we experience will fade. We will be at home in the world. Disciples, however, never feel at home in the world.

THE POWER OF A CREATIVE MINORITY

Jesus attracted crowds; however, Gordon MacDonald reminds us that "Jesus did little to encourage spectators to stick around in crowd formation. Frequently, He seems to have downsized them by enlarging on what it cost to be servants of the real kingdom. The lightweights soon dispersed."[13] We see this approach in the strategy of St. Benedict, who found himself in the midst of a Europe that was in chaos following the fall of the Roman Empire. The structures and institutions that had afforded an era of peace and stability were now gone and with it, learning and order. As chaos grew, St. Benedict withdrew and focused on creating a kind of resilient disciple through monasteries. Benedict placed a challenge before those who would enter his monasteries. There was a high bar. He preferred a few who were committed rather than a crowd who were lax. The commitment of a few would be a foundation upon which to renew a culture. The centrality of a life devoted to Christ would be the foundation upon which to rebuild.

Benedict's monastic retreat could seem like a disengagement from society, but it possessed a missional purpose. In the swirl of cultural and social disorder, these ordered, Christ-centered communities became a kind of oasis. Benedict's monasteries were a spiritual alternative to the castle strongholds that warlords were erecting across Europe in response to the chaos. Christian historian Christopher Dawson observes that Benedict's monasteries operated as an alternative to the clannishness and tribalism that the surrounding culture had reverted to.

The monasteries became centers of learning, which preserved much of the classical knowledge that was being lost. The order of the monasteries, their valuing of work and vocation, their stability and their high moral standing made them attractive places in which trades and business began to flourish. The monasteries were deeply missional and spread across Europe offering a visual and living witness of what the Christian life and community could look like.

> WE SEE JESUS BUILDING HIS MINISTRY UPON GOING DEEP WITH A FEW, RATHER THAN GOING SHALLOW WITH THE PUBLIC.

John Henry Newman likened St. Benedict's monasteries to a kind of revolution of "silent men" who quietly got on with the job of rejuvenating the culture behind the scenes in the most mundane of ways. He writes: "St. Benedict found the world, physical and social, in ruins, and his mission was to restore it. . . . There was no one who contended or cried out, or drew attention to what was going on, but by degrees the woody swamp became a hermitage, a religious house, a farm, an abbey, a village, a seminary, a school of learning and a city."[14]

By going deep with a few, living by code, submitting themselves to God, dwelling in Scripture, and quietly living out the kingdom, the community that gathered around Benedict became magnetic. This wasn't pitch—attractive because it promised immediate benefits; this was something different.

In a time in which chaos and uncertainty dominated, the order, holiness, and devotion of Benedict's community grew in attractiveness. This was a missional move in a time in which Rome had fallen. It was a missional response to a culture corroding and in chaos. Benedict had gone deep with a few, and he then went wide, multiplying the mission of his community by writing a Rule of Life, which guided others who wished to emulate his endeavor. Communities like Benedict's spread across Europe. They not only preserved the essential teaching and discipleship of their faith, but their commitment to learning also preserved many of the fruits of Western culture.

St. Benedict understood that to rebuild a culture and to be a creative minority, one had to return Christ to the center. The flurry of cultural renewal that grew around the monasteries inspired by his rule was built upon understanding our limitations and the limitlessness of God. This order had to be in the correct place. We cannot renew culture and refresh our churches without placing God at the center. We do so by removing ourselves from center stage, by accepting our limitations, by sacrificing and serving. The revolution of release in which we live and the corrosiveness of the third culture can only be answered not by better pitches but by those who are willing to go deep before they go wide.

Chapter 9

Re-create the Institution

A NEW KIND OF "ORGANIZED RELIGION"

The contemporary narrative tells us that a shrinking of the church is linked to the inevitable rise of atheism in developed countries. Yet the statistics across Europe tell another story. In her research into the nature of religious belief in contemporary Europe, religious sociologist Grace Davie notes that "unusually low levels of active religiousness" live alongside "relatively high levels of nominal belief: or to put this into a convenient shorthand, Europe believes but it does not belong."[1]

This is a crucial observation, and I believe that it does not just apply to Europe but across the West, albeit with slightly different contours. The challenge faced by the church in the West is not the rise of unbelief, but rather the rise of a belief that is detached from an idea of belonging. Breaking down the terms, what Davie means by "active religiousness" is concretized, collectivist, creedal belief. What she means by "nominal belief" is a Christian faith that has mutated into a highly individualized, choice-based form. Journalist Damian Thompson also notes this change, not so much in the content of belief, but in how we choose to belong, writing:

> *The deadliest enemy of western Christianity is not Islam or atheism but the infinitely complex process of secularization. Or to put it another way, choice. Long before digital technology, social mobility was undermining what the American scholar of religion Peter Berger calls "plausibility structures"—the networks of people, traditionally your family, friends and neighbors, who believe the same thing as you do. . . . You go away to university and suddenly almost nobody believes what you do, or did. Your siblings move to different towns, so you won't see them in church any more. Your laptop plugs you into any social network that takes your fancy. Even if you're born again as an evangelical Christian, life pushes you from one congregation to another. Many Evangelicals get bored and turn into nones* [nones being those who when asked on a census form of their religion, tick the "none" box]. *The mainstream churches can't cope with this explosion of choice.*
>
> *. . . Religions invariably die, at least on a local level, when no one can be bothered to attend their services.*[2]

Belief is still out there, but it is being renegotiated in order to provide solace while maximizing individual freedom and choice. We want God, but we still want our own authority. A renegotiated Christianity emerges, in which we may still believe, but the nature of our belonging radically changes. This is another legacy of the Gnostic sensibility of our culture.

GNOSTIC CHURCH

The growth of Christians influenced by Gnosticism became one of the great threats that the early church faced. While the shades and details of the Gnostic Christians' theologies varied, their attitude toward the Christian church reflects the prejudices of their philosophy and approach. According to Alister McGrath, the Gnostic Christians "thought of themselves as representing a deeper, more spiritual version of Christianity."[3]

Philip Lee notes that "the Gnostics would have considered bishops, presbyters, and other symbols of discipline, quite acceptable, perhaps even necessary—for ordinary Christians. The idea, however, of the *gnostikoi* having to submit to [ordinariness] was not to be tolerated."[4] It was the ordinariness of church against which the Gnostics bucked. Lee notes that for the Gnostics, "These mundane, uncreative expressions of Christianity so carefully maintained by the orthodox Church were an embarrassment."[5]

The Gnostics complained about having to share Christianity with such unsophisticated and unenlightened folks, and they found the sermons in the orthodox church not intellectually rigorous enough for enlightened and progressing souls as themselves. "Thus the Gnostics felt compelled to separate themselves from the ordinary Christians. Probably most of them remained formally attached to some local Church, took part in some . . . of its activities but meanwhile operated, at least to their own satisfaction, on an entirely different level from the nongnostic members," writes Lee, adding that many simply chose to ignore the sermons and teaching they received in orthodox churches, instead sustaining their Gnostic spiritual journey outside the bounds of enfleshed Christian community with the aid of Gnostic resources.

Some Gnostics left behind the orthodox Christian church to found their own enlightened radical communities, communities shaped by the attitude of superiority that flowed out of the Gnostic idea. Communities of Christ, which gathered around creeds and practiced concrete habits of faith, were an anathema to the Gnostic Christians. Believing individuals were each containers of a divine spark on the road to perfection; any idea of spiritual authority or hierarchy was repulsive to the Gnostics. Authority on early Christian Gnosticism Kurt Rudolph notes that some Gnostics regarded the fabric of the orthodox churches, in their forms, structures, authority, and discipline, as shaped by false ideas that flowed from the authoritarian and flawed inferior god. In contrast, according to the church father Tertullian, the Gnostic Christian communities were rambling, inconsistent, and carelessly administered affairs, in which all enlightened souls were considered equal and unworthy to submit to any kind of spiritual authority or discipline. Other Gnostic Christians simply rejected the church altogether, refusing to believe that something so messy, filled with imperfect humans, could be spiritual. In the Gnostic view, "All . . . institutions are disqualified and regarded as futile for redemption,"[6] writes Rudolph.

With their radical view of human autonomy, the anti-institutional Gnostics were not only post-God but post-church. We see the remnants of this Gnostic prejudice against enfleshed, covenantal forms of faith in today's "organized religion is bad, spirituality is good" sentiment. This residual prejudice not only undermines the potential of such embodied religious communities in our day, but also any other human institutions. The Gnostic bent of our culture has ensured that we are a post-institutional age.

THE UNWINDING

We see the Gnostic effect upon our culture when we look at the health of our institutions. Certain segments of the culture are flourishing. Technology leaps ahead. The fields of style and design move forward at a rapid rate, making the built environment an increasingly beautiful place. Consumerism offers super-abundance, a world of products that are only a click away. Lifestyle industries offer vacations, amazing experiences, and gastronomic delights. Entertainment can provide an endless supply of music, movies, TV shows, live concerts, premium sporting events, and gaming experiences. All of these elements combine to create the buzz, the comfort, and the atmospherics of the beautiful world. They are the industries that fuel and feed our sense of individual autonomy; they provide our pleasures, offering us happiness and stimulation.

However, as the industries of entertainment, image, technology, and consumerism grow, other less glamorous yet vital institutions fade and fall, institutions that were created to foster a sense of community and meaning. Unlike the industries of technology, consumerism, lifestyle, and entertainment, these fading institutions required more than just our money. They asked for commitment. They fostered a sense of duty. They reminded us that freedom needed to be tempered by responsibility and limits, otherwise we would end up as very unhappy and lonely narcissists.

Without realizing it, the church, like so many other institutions in our culture, has been caught in tension between the rise of individual autonomy and the unraveling of social institutions. Journalist George Packer calls this phenomenon "the Unwinding," a process in which the communal ties, institutions, and commitments that bind us together have begun to unwind in an unprecedented process. This unwinding occurs at the same time as our individual freedom grows. Packer writes:

> The unwinding brings freedom, more than the world has ever granted, and to more kinds of people than ever before—freedom to go away, freedom to return, freedom to change your story, get your facts, get hired, get fired, get high, marry, divorce, go broke, begin again, start a business, have it both ways, take it to the limit, walk away from the ruins, succeed beyond your dreams and boast about it, fail abjectly and try again. And with freedom the unwinding brings its illusions, for all these pursuits are as fragile as thought balloons popping against circumstances.

> *This much freedom leaves you on your own. More Americans than*
> *ever before live alone, but even a family can exist in isolation, just*
> *managing to survive in the shadow of a huge military base without a*
> *soul to lend a hand. A shiny new community can spring up overnight*
> *miles from anywhere, then fade away just as fast. An old city can lose*
> *its industrial foundation and two-thirds of its people, while all its*
> *mainstays—churches, government, businesses, charities, unions—fall*
> *like building flats in a strong wind, hardly making a sound. Alone on a*
> *landscape without solid structures, Americans have to improvise their*
> *own destinies, plot their own stories of success and salvation.*[7]

Packer's book follows the lives of a number of people over the last forty years. Some ordinary, some famous, all who have had to navigate the terrain between unprecedented freedom and the fading of institutions, communities, and projects that gave people meaning. Whereas many see the '60s as a tumultuous decade of social change, after which slowly Western culture returned to a kind of normality, Packer sees the decade as a preface to an ongoing, rolling crisis in our culture as the core institutions of our society have been wounded, some irreparably, by the rise of individual selfishness. This crisis has seen the incredible diminishment of communal activities, not just in churches but across the board.

Robert Putnam, in his much-read book *Bowling Alone*, notes the loss since the '60s of widespread engagement in voluntary associations, be they political, religious, community, recreational, or altruistic. "Somehow in the last several decades of the twentieth century all these community groups and tens of thousands like them . . . began to fade."[8]

Interestingly, just like the church, Putnam notices that as attendance began to fall and commitment began to wane, many of these groups presumed the problem lay with them. Reports and inquiries began to search for the key to reform that would revive the institution.

However, larger forces within culture were shifting. Putnam notes that people had more time on their hands yet were less inclined to spend it civically or communally. Radical individualism and healthy institutions struggled to coexist. When it comes to combating poverty in the Two-Thirds World, experts overwhelmingly agree that a lack of healthy institutions or lack of institutions altogether is one of the biggest factors to making people poor. Disease, terrorism, illegal drug production, and trafficking thrive in cultures in which institutions are failing or fallen.

After their exhaustive global study of why some nations fall into poverty and chaos while other nations are peaceful and prosperous, Daron Acemoglu and James Robinson answer the question, "Why do nations fail?" "Institutions, institutions, institutions."[9] Yet while the West encourages developing countries to improve their lives and cultures by strengthening their institutions, historian Niall Ferguson, in his book *The Great Degeneration,*[10] notes that the institutions of the West are degenerating. Alongside the self-interest that has become rampant within private lives within the West, self-interest has become endemic within institutions. This decay has resulted in a growing cynicism as public trust in key institutions fades and in some cases disappears altogether. This cynicism creates an excuse to retreat from public engagement and civil society. We retreat into the world of self-interest, failing to see that it was self-interest that compromised institutions; we prefer to disconnect from them altogether.

OUR NEW NETWORKED REALITY

It would seem logical that our retreat from institutions, wisdom, and relationships would leave us feeling vulnerable, yet a number of factors give the illusion of mitigating these losses. Technology continues to advance. The bounty of consumer culture seems to offer a huge variety of distractions or solutions to the loss of meaning and stability.

Inevitably when moments of doubt occur that our ideology of personal freedom seems ultimately a selfish position, when our wills find that there are limits to what they can achieve, the cult of "personal rights" reeducates the individual back to the orthodoxy of radical individualism.

The existential fear of a world of boundless individuals unprotected by institutions and binding relationships is also downplayed by the new language of networks and systems. This new viewpoint attempts to replace the solidity of institutions with the fluidity and flexibility of networks. Despite our infatuation with networks, as Malcolm Gladwell reminds us, they cannot replace institutions:

> There are many things, though, that networks don't do well. Car companies sensibly use a network to organize their hundreds of suppliers, but not to design their cars. No one believes that the articulation of a coherent design philosophy is best handled by a sprawling, leaderless organizational system. Because networks don't have a centralized leadership structure and clear lines of authority, they have real difficulty reaching consensus and setting goals. They can't think strategically; they are chronically prone to conflict and error. How do you make difficult choices about tactics or strategy or philosophical direction when everyone has an equal say? . . . The drawbacks of networks scarcely matter if the network isn't interested in systemic change—if it just wants to frighten or humiliate or make a splash—or if it doesn't need to think strategically. But if you're taking on a powerful and organized establishment you have to be a hierarchy.[11]

Our current fascination of and preference for networks ultimately stems from our unspoken belief that they are the best organizing principle for a culture in which the individual will is paramount. This is the gospel of Silicon Valley. In contrast, institutions require discipline, compromise, conflict and conflict resolution, and a limit on our will. We prefer to believe that we are all simply equally placed nodules in a network, with no binding relational commitments required of us, apart from "adding friends" or "following" users; that each one of us has an equal say, that opinion can be given without responsibility. In the structural entity that we know of as an institution there is responsibility that flows upwards and downwards. Institutions have goals, directions, and shared cultures. The network on the other hand is driven by no story, it is filled with endless possibilities, it is marked by randomness. Just look at your Twitter or Facebook feed for ten minutes, a chaotic mix of personal opinion, factoids, unconnected experiences, and breaking news.

IS CHURCH AN INSTITUTION?

The reduction in church attendance cannot be attributed simply to the growth of secularism or to the church's own self-inflicted wounds. Yes, these factors count, but the church, alongside other institutions, has been caught in our culture's Gnostic repulsion against institutions and enfleshed communities. Ray Ortlund observes, "To call anything an 'institution' today can be its death sentence, including a church. Should we be ashamed of the institutional aspects of our churches?" Ortlund notes that we should reject not institutions but rather institutionalization:

> An institution is a social mechanism where life-giving human activities can be nurtured and protected and sustained. Some aspects of life should be unscheduled, spontaneous, random. But not all of life should be. What an institution does is structure a desirable experience, so that it becomes repeatable on a regular basis. Institutions are not a problem. But institutionalization is. An institution is meant to enrich life. But institutionalization takes that good thing and turns it into death. How? The institutional structure, the mechanism, takes on its own inherent purpose.[12]

OUR DANGER IS NOT TO LOOK TO INSTITUTIONS TO SAVE US, BUT RATHER TO LOOK TO OURSELVES TO SAVE US.

Throughout history, in other places in the world, and indeed in some places within the West, people face the problem of institutionalization. Some churches have degenerated from healthy institutions into institutionalization. However, the problem we are tackling in this book is the problem not of institutions taking on their own inherent purpose as Ortlund states it, but when individuals run rogue with their own purposes. It is worth noting that one can make the error of looking to institutions to save us. The twentieth century saw millions sacrifice their lives to totalitarian regimes, demonic institutions run amok—however, this is not our temptation today. We live in a post-institutional age. Our danger is not to look to institutions to save us, but rather to look to ourselves to save us.

AN UNGHOSTLY PEOPLE

God called Israel to be holy yet divinely solid, a walking, communal incarnation of God's intent to break into history with life-giving salvation. In other lands, philosophers also wrestled with theories of divine spirit and dirt. Many wished to leave the world behind, to cast off the chains of dirt and matter, and to melt into the Gnostic embrace of the purely spiritual. Others, repelled by the seeming distance of the spiritual, wished instead to enjoy life in the dirt, to eke out of the muck and mud pleasures and distraction, while the decay of our mortality eventually overtook us.

Yet in Israel we see afresh the coming together of spirit and earth. The worship that God would call Israel to would scale the heights of transcendence, and at the same time, its commandments reached into the most earthly of human matters. The Scriptures of Israel could contain prophetic, ethereal visions of the heavenly court, alongside commandments regarding menstrual blood, ethical outpourings for justice alongside erotically charged verse, and psalms filled with praise, tears, anger, and joy. This was no "spirituality." This was a blood and guts religion that did not tolerate a distance between heart and mind, word and deed. It was a world of commitments and connections, a universe of relationships and responsibilities.

We are so used to philosophies that elevate spirit over earth or earth over spirit that we struggle to understand how the two could be combined, let alone used by God. This is part of the reason we struggle with institutions or the institutional elements of church or Christian life. We prefer the communal and the relational to the institutional and the organizational. This false dichotomy can be traced back to the German sociologist Ferdinand Tönnies, who used two different German words to describe two forms of human association.[13] In English the words were translated into *society* and *community*. Thus in our minds there is the false division that ultimately there are two types of organizations possible: "community," which is rich, relational, communal, spiritual, and rewarding, and "society," which is institutional, administrational, organized, and impersonal.

However, no such divide existed in Israel nor exists within the church today. Israel then was solid, as well as spiritual, as T. F. Torrance writes:

> By elaborate religious rituals and carefully framed laws, by rivers of blood from millions of animal sacrifices, by the broken hearts of the psalmists and the profoundest agony of the prophets, by the tragic story of Israelite politics and the shattering of this people again and again and again, God taught the Jews, through centuries and centuries of existence yoked to his word and covenant, until it was burned into their souls, the meaning of holiness and righteousness, of sin and uncleanness, of love and mercy and grace, of faithfulness and forgiveness, of justification, atonement, and salvation; the meaning of creation, the kingdom of God, of judgment, death, and at last resurrection; the

concept of the Messiah, the suffering servant, and yet prophet, priest and king, and so to the very brink of the gospel.[14]

As Torrance notes, we are not at the gospel; we are at the very brink of the gospel. Israel was an environment, a creedal community, that provided freedoms and limitations, restrictions and rituals. However, her rules, rituals, and regulations could not justify Israel. As Paul writes, these were for the Jews "our guardian until Christ, so that we could be justified by faith" (Galatians 3:24). The foundation was a guardian from the imprisonment of being totally unrestrained, against injustice and self-interest, a protection against sin of self, sin of others. The limitations of the creedal community of Israel were a solid reminder that the people were not God. Israel was not a tool for self-creation and the pursuit of ultimate autonomy. The concreteness of Israel, as Torrance writes, took them to the brink of the gospel by showing them how much they needed God.

We buck and resist the institutional, creedal, restrictive, sacrificial elements of church life because ultimately we have been formed to self-create. To self-create one needs freedom, no responsibility, nothing mundane, no binding relationships or communal commitments; just free space in which to indulge our fantasies of our own godlikeness. Such fantasies cannot be entertained in the institutional realities of creedal communities. Institutions serve us well by reminding us that we are not God. Gnostic believers are ultimately anti-institutional believers who see no purpose in the benefits that institutions can bring. Let's begin to explore the benefits that institutions, in particular Christian institutions, bring us.

INSTITUTIONS ARE BELIEFS ENFLESHED

Institutions are our beliefs and ethics enfleshed. They bring ideas down from the ether and ensure that they are operating within the actual life of a community. They are creedal in nature. They are a shared set of beliefs upon which a society can agree and define itself by. They exist to ensure that we put our beliefs into practice. In order to transform our beliefs and ethics into actual behavior, institutions must pass on values and educate. This is more than just the transferring of information. The great American sociologist Robert Nisbet noted that institutions don't educate others just with information but with values.[15] Nisbet observed that values, such as love and loyalty, must be passed on within relational framework of smaller institutions, most notably the family. When institutions decay and die, the transmission of values is replaced by the broadcasting of information; no longer is wisdom passed on, but only novelty.

To embody a community's beliefs, institutions must contain commands. If the established values of a community are to be enacted, it is not enough that we vaguely pay adherence to these core values, but we must shape our lives and actions around them. Institutions have to instruct us what to do. They must contain commands. These commands may mean short-term sacrifice, but they will ensure freedom, human flourishing, and peace, so we obey to benefit. If there are commands, there also must be prohibitions and regulations that prevent behaviors that the institution believes will harm the collective and the individual, or the institution itself. Institutions thus require the individual to at some point submit to the authority of the institution with its commands and controls to enjoy a flourishing that they could not achieve on their own.

> HEALTHY INSTITUTIONS ARE A WAY OF LEARNING FROM THE PAST AND CREATING A BETTER FUTURE.

The universal nature of institutions, in which anyone can join if they are willing to submit to the commands and regulations, is a natural guard against tribalism, nepotism, and special interest groups dominating. Institutions act as safeguards. The institution of the rule of law, alongside regulatory bodies, exists to protect the community against corruption and damaging self-interest. They exist to protect us from our own sinful natures, while ensuring that we flourish both collectively and individually. Healthy institutions are participatory—yes, they have commands and regulation, but they also allow us a voice. They require that we take part, that we be engaged members.

THE PARTNERSHIP OF THE GENERATIONS

When the Asian tsunami of 2004 hit Aceh in Indonesia, over 167,000 people tragically died. Yet on the island of Simeulue just off Aceh only seven people perished. Why? The answer was an institution on the island of Simeulue called *smong*. It is a storytelling tradition in which elders tell stories to the children of the island. Every smong story ends with this warning: "If a strong tremor occurs, and if the sea withdraws soon after, run to the hills, for the sea will soon rush ashore."[16] So when a strong tremor occurred and the sea withdrew, everybody upon the island knew the gravity of the situation and what to do. If the storytelling institution of smong had not been treated with the utmost seriousness and consciousness, it could have easily been lost. Self-interest and the lack of a living memory of such an event occurring could have easily led to the tradition being abandoned, but the commands of the institutions remained strong and lives were saved. It was the investment of the past, through the transmission of wisdom into the future.

The institution of smong is what Edmund Burke called the partnership of the generations; that is, the idea that institutions give voice and place to those who have died and those yet to be born. This idea seems strange to us today, so entrenched in our personal perspective, but healthy institutions should—if they are truly healthy—outlive us. They are a way of learning from the past and creating a better future. The voices of the past provide us wisdom, they can show us where the dangerous rocks lie, they can teach us the principles, beliefs, and values that operate in any time or context. The wisdom of those who went before us teaches us to think long term, to see beyond just the instant. The value of the wisdom passed on to us by past generations encourages us to wonder what our contribution to the next generation will be.

As Andy Crouch writes, "Institutions are the way the teeming abundance of human creativity and culture are handed on to future generations."[17] The thought that after us comes another generation who will inherit both our mistakes and our successes is a sobering one. It is hard to be a selfish person when you know that another coming generation may have to pay the price for your own self-interest. Israel was commanded in Deuteronomy, "Do this so that you may fear the Lord your God all the days of your life by keeping all His statutes and commands I am giving you, your son, and your grandson" (6:2). This was the partnership of the generations, a constant investing into the future.

Jesus commanded His followers to "go, therefore, and make disciples of all nations, baptizing them in the name of the Father and of the Son and of the Holy Spirit, teaching them to observe everything I have commanded you" (Matthew 28:19–20). This also is the partnership of the generations. Those disciples went out into the world and invested in the future; they discipled someone who discipled someone, across seas, cultures, and nations, centuries and millennia, all the way to you today.

INSTITUTIONS LIMIT US

Institutions remind us of our limitations, that we are not the Messiah; rather that Jesus is the Messiah, for we live under the lordship of a Messiah who is to return and complete His plan for the redemption of the world. In this in-between time, our flesh battles with our spirit.

This runs against our learned grain. We prefer to think of ourselves only battling against the limits and prohibitions set before us, foot soldiers in the revolution of release. Ruth Haley Barton observes that the apostle Paul, in a passage advising the church in Corinth on how to live within the institution of the church, praises limitations. Paul notes that some people wish to expand their own personal boundaries by boasting, taking the credit for that which is outside of their authority. "His antidote for this all-too-human tendency was to stay within the limits of his own life and calling,"[18] writes Barton.

Paul writes: "We, however will not boast beyond measure but according to the measure of the area of ministry that God has assigned to us. . . . For we are not overextending ourselves . . . since we have come to you with the gospel of Christ" (2 Corinthians 10:13–14).

Each of us has been given an area by God within which to work. We are placed in a context, in a community, in institutions and webs of responsibility. And Paul is reminding us that this is good. The script of our culture tells us that we can only find self-fulfillment when we break away from these limitations, but Paul is reversing that false view of life. Limitations and the defined space of living and ministering that God gives us within the institution of the church is a gift. God places us in institutions, relationships, responsibilities, to teach us and shape us into Christlikeness. Barton writes,

MAYBE WE NEED TO REIMAGINE CHURCH AS A SPIRITUAL DISCIPLINE.

> One of the ways to recognize narcissism within ourselves is to notice when we have not yet accepted the field, the sphere of action, that God has given us—the opportunities and the limits of life in this body, this community, this set of relationships . . . this place where we have been called by God to serve. Narcissistic leaders are always looking longingly at someone else's field as somehow more worthy or more indicative of

success. They are always pushing the limits of their situation rather than lovingly working the field they have been given. . . . Our unwillingness to live within limits—both personally and in community—is one of the deepest sources of depletion and eventual burnout. That's the bad news.[19]

Our culture is depleted and burned out because it rebels against the God-given limitations placed on it. Individuals are depleted because we refuse to live within the fields that God has given us. Instead, we burn ourselves out seeking greater freedom and autonomy. Barton reminds us, "The good news is that there is something deeply spiritual about living and working within our God-ordained limits—or to put it another way, living fully and acceptingly within our own set of realities."[20]

In an age that encourages maximum autonomy and the transgressing of limitations, perhaps we need to adhere to Todd Hunter's advice to see the institution of church as a spiritual discipline.[21] We get the idea that making the choice to wake up early and read our Bibles or to commit to regularly giving away our money to a charity or to fast may not always be pleasurable, but in the discipline of these things that we become more Christlike. Yet we expect church to always be pleasurable, enriching, and exciting.

Maybe the limitations of church, the discipline of regular attendance, the commitment it requires, also teach us to be Christlike. Maybe we need to reimagine church in our minds as a spiritual discipline, which teaches us the value of delayed gratification, of personally investing in change, of becoming more like Jesus.

Ronald Rolheiser captures this truth well when he writes, "Church involvement, when understood properly, does not leave us the option to walk away whenever something happens that we do not like. It is a covenant commitment, like a marriage, and binds us for better or worse." We and our Gnostic predilections ultimately fear church because we fear that it will take something from us, that it will restrict us. And on this point the Gnostics, both ancient and modern, are right. For as Rolheiser writes, "What church community takes away from us is our false freedom to soar unencumbered, like the birds, believing that we are mature, loving, committed, and not blocking out things that we should be seeing. Real churchgoing soon enough shatters this illusion, and gives us no escape, as we find ourselves constantly humbled as our immaturities and lack of sensitivity to the pain of others are reflected off eyes that are honest and unblinking." Ultimately, we fear church because it crushes Christian Gnostics, who pick their bruised and beaten bodies up, and discover that they are not gods, but humans fearfully and wonderfully made.

The rebellious trajectory of Gnostic individualism ultimately destroys community. Satan and the fallen angels' pursuit of autonomy apart from God fractured the heavenly court, Adam and Eve's attempt to be as God fractured creation, and our Gnostic rebellion to take from church while maximizing our individual autonomy fractures our churches today. However, the imprint of the cross upon the church means that as we receive grace along its vertical axis, we must encounter and share grace with those alongside of it, both to and through friend and alien. This is the gift of grace that flows from Christ soaking the church.

Any responses to secularism that do not contain resilient, enfleshed, communal forms of faith will be eroded into ghostliness by the superabundance of choice. As Rolheiser comments, "Our age tends to divorce spirituality from ecclesiology. We want God, but we don't want church." However, the great flaw of our search for spirituality and faith minus church is "the unconfronted life. Without church, we have more private fantasy than real faith. . . . Real conversion demands that eventually its recipient be involved in both the muck and the grace of actual church life."[22] More than ever we need the limitations and glorious messiness of church. We need its relational concreteness. We need it because it is the vehicle, in all its warts and spots, of the grace of God. The mere fact that God chooses it, in the same way that He chooses us, humble vessels, is part of His grace that fools the wisdom of the world.

THE POTENTIAL OF A MARGINALIZED CHURCH IN THE BEAUTIFUL WORLD

Yet this grace that fools the wisdom of the world is often not served well by the strategy of relevance. The language of "relevant" and "irrelevant" ministry reduces the posture of the church to either one of complete engagement or total withdrawal. However, when the church comprehends its role as a creative minority, new possibilities emerge.

In his book *David and Goliath*, the wildly popular author Malcolm Gladwell both shares the story of his rediscovered Christian faith and powerfully illustrates the counterintuitive truth that in a struggle, the advantage often lies with the underdog. Gladwell cites the work of the political scientist Ivan Arreguin-Toft, who calculated that in the past two centuries when a larger country has engaged a smaller country in warfare, the larger country wins about 70 percent of the time. However, when the smaller, less powerful country employs unconventional tactics, the advantage swings to the underdog, with weaker nations winning about 60 percent of the time. The great Chinese sage of conflict Sun-Tzu also understood the concept, calling it "death ground," noting that a smaller force could defeat a larger force if they were fighting for their lives. The old adage stands: It is not the size of the dog in the fight, but the size of the fight in the dog.

For the foreseeable future the church will be the smaller dog in the West. Yet if Gladwell is right, instead of mourning our marginal position, we should embrace our cultural exile, recognizing that within it there are advantages to be discovered, if only we look with the right eyes. As Gladwell states, "We spend a lot of time thinking about the ways that prestige and resources and belonging to elite institutions make us better off. We don't spend enough time thinking about the ways in which those kinds of material advantages limit our options."[23]

What if our attempts at relevance, at mimicking and outdoing the beautiful world, actually limit our ministry potential? What if our increasing strangeness to Western culture is actually to our advantage? What if the fact that you can no longer be warmly embraced in the contemporary cultural fold if you are an orthodox Christian is actually the best thing that has happened to us?

Both Gladwell and Arreguin-Toft point to the example of T. E. Lawrence, more famously known as Lawrence of Arabia, as a prime example of the power and potential of the underdog. Lawrence, an archaeologist, was viewed as a weird eccentric even by those who knew him well. His personality and manner could not have been further from the expected behavior of a British officer. Yet Lawrence would play a vital role in the First World War, leading the great Arab revolt against the Ottoman Empire. Lawrence's efforts and leadership abilities would lead Winston Churchill to proclaim that he was the greatest human being of his time. But because the British government was unsure what to do with such an oddball, Lawrence was sent not to the Western Front in France but to the backwater of the Middle East, with little funding, equipment, support, or training. Yet as Gladwell notes, it was precisely because Lawrence had little investment in the status quo of the military establishment that he was able to operate so effectively in the foreign terrain of the Middle East. Whereas other military men on both sides assigned to the region viewed the area as a constant challenge to their usual practices, Lawrence adapted to the environment, choosing to see opportunity where others saw obstacles. He understood that history is moved from the margins.

It is important not to lionize Lawrence—the man was far from a saint—yet I believe that we need to think like Lawrence in our struggle. To see advantage where others see disadvantage. For there are a number of advantages that the church enjoys, marginalized in our beautiful world.

EMBRACING THE CLOAK OF INVISIBILITY

Lawrence biographer Scott Anderson asks a vital question: "How did he do it? How did a painfully shy Oxford archaeologist without a single day of formal military training become the battlefield commander of a foreign revolutionary army, the master political strategist who foretold many of the Middle East calamities to come? The short answer might seem anticlimactic: Lawrence was able to become 'Lawrence of Arabia' because no one was paying much attention."[24]

> MAYBE WITH THE CULTURAL SPOTLIGHT ELSEWHERE, WE CAN GET ON WITH THE BUSINESS OF BEING THE CHURCH.

Part of the pain of our post-Christian age is found in its habit of ignoring and marginalizing Christianity, seeing the whole endeavor as irrelevant. Yet maybe, just as Lawrence found an advantage in the fact that no one was paying any attention, we also will discover the power of cultural invisibility. For we follow the Christ who ran from the crowd, whose saving death upon the cross took place on a garbage dump witnessed by a few. Maybe with the spotlight elsewhere, like the early church that was mostly ignored as the crowd flocked to its bread and circuses, we can get on with the business of being the church. Of preaching the good news, discipling, worshiping, helping the poor, building Christian community. What if being a city on a hill is not about broadcasting with the bright spotlights of the day, but rather allowing the world to be bathed in the gentle, magnetic glow of the kingdom?

THE POWER OF REAL PEOPLE

What if ordinary ministry and Christian practice offers a rare opportunity in our day—a genuine encounter and engagement with real people? In a world where friends are added with a button and the beautiful, blank faces of stock photography stare out at us, church and faith offer us true, face-to-face encounters.

For English philosopher Roger Scruton,[25] one of the great weaknesses of contemporary atheistic Western culture is its inability to offer a genuine concept of personhood. It cannot truly explain to us why the human face, why human relationships, why human music and art move us so. What if a great advantage is that in our strange and sometimes awkward gatherings and groupings, the church can offer the gift of facilitating human relationship along its entire bandwidth of connection from the superficially social to the deeply spiritual? Relationships centered around what Scruton notes all faces point toward—the face of God?

THE POWER OF STRONG TIES

Churches that recognize the power of real people must also harness the power of strong ties. Sociologists note that there are two kinds of relationships that make up networks: weak ties and strong ties. Social networking is brilliant at reaching and even multiplying weak ties. Yet deep social change occurs when strong ties are built and mobilized. Strong ties are committed, long-term, intimate, reciprocal, sacrificial.

In an age where we have cheap tools and technologies to grow churches and ministries rapidly through weak ties, we can forget that the church has always grown through strong ties. Rodney Stark, the sociologist of religion, has researched the explosive growth of the early church[26] and notes the power of strong ties, for when someone was transformed by the gospel those who had strong ties to them could not help but be affected by this change. Strong ties are not easy to develop and nurture; they are hard to develop programs around and harder to measure, yet in a world of increasingly weak ties they are one of the great advantages to be harnessed by the church in the West.

THE SCIENCE OF SIN

I am a big fan of the films of Alfred Hitchcock, not just for his craft, but for his ability to make us see the sin and chaos that lurks underneath all of us. Hitchcock made films during a time in which Britain and America had just fought a war against Nazism and were involved in a cold war against Stalinist Communism. Evil was seen as "out there," in foreign lands, in rabid and destructive ideologies. Yet Hitchcock's deft cinematic hand pulled back the curtain in our own potential for evil, for duplicity, deceit, and sin. Again in our time, fractiously divided between left and right, conservatives and progressives, feverishly we point out evil on the "other side." Yet Christianity illustrates, as the Russian novelist Alexander Solzhenitsyn noted, that the line between good and evil runs through the human heart. We the church, more than ever, must show the humility that comes from knowing that we are flawed and fallen.

BUILDING INNER LIVES

A world centered on image, the distraction of constant entertainment, and the projection of a successful self is a world where the inner life wilts. One of the great ministry challenges I have faced in recent years is pastorally caring for people who on the surface seem to have it all but who live with a poverty of an inner life, It does not take much more than a quick dip into the platitudes of fridge magnet philosophy, and the Gnostic-like advice of many self-help books, to grasp the fact that the culture we live in does not offer much on which

143

to build a deep inner life. The gospel transforms us from the inside out. The resilience, peace, depth, and wisdom that following Christ gives our inner lives are resources sorely needed in our day. Churches are the place where in community we discover inner depth.

A GRAND, COHERENT STORY

In a confused and contradictory world, the grand theme of Scripture offers a coherent worldview. Instead of the choppy narrative of the single-person play, the gospel invites us into God's great story, of which our singular part contributes to the great mosaic of salvation beauty, in which we are invited to partner with the Creator Himself in the redemption of the world and the marriage of heaven and earth. This story, even whispered between people on a suburban train, is grander and more resonant than the biggest-budget Hollywood blockbuster or the cleverest viral marketing campaign.

MORE THAN ME

On our church signs, our tagline—"More Than Me"—is larger than the name of our church, Red Church. This is a deliberate move; early on we felt that in an age of "me-ism" it was important to convey the poignancy and punch of the good news of Jesus' death and resurrection, showing us that the way to discover true life is by giving up our lives. In the gospel we encounter God, who gives us life that we may live. Jesus' work upon the cross invites us into a life that is built upon submission and surrender to God. Nothing is as comforting and confronting as the gospel's message that life is about more than me. Thus, in a culture based upon radical individual authority, Jesus' sacrificial death is the church's ultimate guide as we fight our unconventional struggle.

Chapter 10

Withdraw/Return

WHEN THE AVALANCHE HITS

The 2014 film *Force Majeure* features a Swedish family on a skiing holiday in the French Alps. The attractive parents in their thirties, in their matching smart casual wear, are exemplary citizens of the beautiful world. The artificiality of the ski resort they are staying in with its sleek design, automatic walkways, and snowmaking machines mirrors the artificiality of the family. Representing the modern, egalitarian Scandinavian family, the father Tomas's parental role is reduced to being the provider of the Internet password for his children's tablets. The family has taken the vacation so that Tomas can spend more time with his children, yet although physically present, he is absent, lost in his phone. His only way of relating to his children is through letting them play with his drone. The family are surprised that an American that they meet believes in God. In their controlled, designed world, mirrored by the controlled, insulated world of the ski lodge, there is seemingly no need for God.

As the family breakfast in an open-air restaurant, a controlled avalanche in the distance gains their attention. Tomas begins filming with his iPhone, reassuring his family that there is nothing to be worried about as the avalanche picks up force moving toward them at an increasing pace. Then in a second, a spectacle becomes an imminent danger as the rush of snow moves dangerously close. Tomas's young son Harry screams in fear as the avalanche hits. As the diners are showered in snow, Tomas instinctively grabs his iPhone, and sprints. Pushing over other people in his way. Abandoning his family. *Force Majeure* refers to a French legal term referring to an act of God. The avalanche—the act of God—shatters their illusions of control and comfort.

Moments later, the diners register that they are okay, there are no injuries, they have simply been showered in snow. Once the cloud of snow has passed, Tomas returns to the table, the family continues eating. Physically there is no damage, yet Tomas's actions have changed things irrevocably. Later that night, dining with another couple, Tomas's wife Ebba, in the middle of conversation, raises Tomas's actions during the avalanche. Awkward and uncomfortable laughter masks her disappointment with him. It is as if Tomas and Ebba, raised in a comfortable, controlled world, have no language with which to describe how Tomas's actions have unmasked unspoken expectations about roles, character, and virtue.

As the children withdraw further from their father into their screens, as Ebba rejects Tomas's amorous advances, the family begins to experience their own interpersonal avalanche. Tomas's friend, who has joined the family, attempts to reassure him that modern males should no longer feel the pressure to be heroic. Valor, he argues, belongs to an older epoch. Tomas's tactic is to deny that he ran; however, after Ebba replays the video he shot on his iPhone, there is no doubt. Tomas finally breaks down in guilt, confessing that he is pathetic. That he has cheated on Ebba, and that he even cheats on the children during board games. Sobbing, he claims that Ebba and the children are not the only victims, that he himself is a victim of his own instincts.

Ebba meets a fellow Swede at the resort, who is also a mother like her. Ebba discovers that she is alone, taking a break from her children and marriage to sleep with strangers at the resort. The woman explains that she and her husband have progressed to an open relationship, which allows them personal autonomy, and the freedom to pursue their own desires. Ebba struggles as she emotionally reacts to this mode of living. She is reaching and grasping for a morality that she senses in herself, but cannot articulate or even readily accept.

As they struggle to hold their family and their emotions together, it is easy to judge them, to take pleasure as their comfortable and selfish world falls apart. Yet as I watched a question popped into my head. How would you disciple Tomas and Ebba?

DISCIPLING TOMAS

How would you minister to, or reach out to, these lost souls who have had no role models? Who live in a godless world, which offers progressive values divorced from the upside-down kingdom of Christ? Who rightly can claim that they are victims of their own instincts and desires but they have only ever been told to pursue and satiate them? Who are distanced from acts of God, death, suffering, and poverty? Who have no workable idea of the good, of virtues, of character, of the development of an inner life? Who don't know the freedom of grace and surrender?

Straddling the two worlds of writing about culture and spending my days pastoring in a secular, progressive environment, I can intellectually critique and interpret the cultural forces that have created the Tomases and Ebbas of the beautiful world, but as a pastor, I know what it is to sit with the Tomases. To minister to fragile and anxious Ebbas. To hear the lostness of people who have no inner life. People who have been groomed by media, web 2.0, and hyper-consumerism, in what Daniel Goleman calls "the reign of impulse,"[1] in which sophisticated and subtle techniques are used to shape our impulses and desires. People who are manipulated to believe that the beautiful world will turn up for them one day, only then to encounter frustration, pain, and depression.

Reflecting upon the task of ministering to or discipling a Tomas or Ebba, I realized that a greater question is before us. For the Tomases and Ebbas of the beautiful world are not just outside the boundaries of the church. As the impending avalanche of secularism approaches, are we like Tomas, distracted by our phones? Are we disconnectedly simply filming the event, offering opinion from afar? Maybe we are like Ebba, horrified and frightened by what we see, maternally grabbing our children in an attempt to shield them from the onslaught, as we are engulfed.

THE ENEMY IS NOT OUTSIDE THE RAMPARTS, IT IS INSIDE THE CASTLE.

More disturbingly we must ask, are we like Tomas, running for our own lives, eschewing our God-given mandate and authority, pushing others out of the way, while saving our own skin? After teaching at an event about the way in which our cultural climate encourages narcissism, I was approached by a young woman. She had appreciated my talk but was concerned. When it came to the disturbing cultural trends that I was outlining, such as self-promotion, insecurity, and self-obsession, the worst offenders in her experience were pastors, Christian activists, and thought leaders. As she spoke I sensed that she was not cynically taking a potshot, she was looking for answers, and yet those who were meant to be modeling an alternative seemed to simply mirror the values of the culture. The enemy is not outside the ramparts, it is inside the castle. The real issue is not about doing mission and ministry to the Tomases of the beautiful world, but that we have become Tomas ourselves.

THE CROWD SAPS OUR COURAGE

Tomas's abandonment of his family is made easier as the crowd of diners around him panic, scream, and scramble for safety. Nothing erodes courage like a crowd. One Christmas Eve I was making some last-minute purchases at a packed store when the fire alarm began to sound. No one vacated the building; instead we all exchanged glances noticing that no one else was moving, and continued on with our shopping. Next came an announcement over the sirens that we should leave by the exits. Again no one left the store; a powerful feedback loop was in operation. Until it was broken by an individual going against the crowd and heading for the exits, we were stuck; the crowd was the ultimate authority.

The situation then became even more surreal as smoke began to move across the ceiling. Still no one moved, the power of the crowd stayed strong. Finally, staff from the store had to herd us out of the building. A small fire had broken out in a kitchen, which was easily dealt with by the fire brigade, and as I drove home I reflected on how stupid I was to not leave the building when the first alarm sounded, and just how powerful the effect of the crowd is upon us.

In our age of media and social networking the crowd is even more powerful. Like the feedback loop created in the store that day, we look to each other for opinion and reinforcement. The great irony of our age of radical individuals is that we become more enslaved by the collective. Secularism represents a shift from the vertical authority of God to the horizontal authority of the crowd. The writer of Hebrews, in chapter 11, paints a vast canvas of faith, reaching back into Israel's past. The process of following God along the ancient path of faith through generations is illuminated for all to see. At the end of the chapter we are told, "They went about in sheepskins and goatskins, destitute, persecuted and mistreated—the world was not worthy of them. They wandered in deserts and mountains, living in caves and in holes in the ground" (Hebrews 11:37–38 NIV). Those who walk the path of faith find themselves retreating from the world to serve it.

RESILENT INFLUENCERS

A church that does not disappear in the soil of the third culture is a church that is composed of and that produces extremeophile (remember the trees that thrived) believers. In *Resilience*,[2] their study of why systems, networks, and organizations survive and develop resilience, Andrew Zolli and Ann Marie Healy found that at the center of resilient systems were certain kinds of leaders who were both resilient and promoted resilience in those around them. We see in both Scripture and the history of the church: God has allowed men and women to enter into extreme environments, to be tested to their absolute limits, to face isolation and opposition. Through this process these disciples emerge as kinds of extremeophiles of faith, who become models of how to follow God faithfully and flourish in challenging environments.

Such Christ-followers tend to be formed by a process the British historian Arnold J. Toynbee called "Withdraw/Return."[3] As I have reflected on the process and explored the way that it shapes disciples, I began to notice that when God takes people through Withdraw/Return it not only shapes their inner world, it also offers a kind of cultural key, one that can bring life and healing to others. I think in my first exploration of the process I was focused upon the Withdraw and missed the importance of the Return, and the cultural key that can be discovered and passed onto others. Toynbee saw the principle of Withdraw/Return most clearly in the prophets of the Bible, and in Jesus Himself.

CALVIN AND IGNATIUS

Two such men, whose followers were often rivals yet who shaped their time in incredible ways, were John Calvin and Ignatius of Loyola. Both wished for a very different life than the life God would give them. Ignatius was a playboy soldier who foresaw ahead of him a life of military glory; Calvin wished for a quiet, scholarly life. Both men would find themselves moving through the process of Withdraw/Return. Ignatius's withdrawal was instantly and violently caused by a cannonball, which rendered him disabled. This physical impediment sent him on a journey toward total submission to God, eventually leading him on a pilgrimage to Jerusalem. Calvin would be forced to flee the Catholic authorities in his homeland in France, and find refuge in the Swiss Protestant republic of Geneva. We will use the lives of both Calvin and Ignatius to illustrate the process of how God forms leaders through Withdraw/Return. We can also use these men to discover cultural keys—ideas and themes that will resonate with a particular group.

1) WITHDRAW

A retreat. A distancing from what is known and comfortable. An exile. A wilderness. A breach with the surrounding culture.

Ignatius and Calvin were born into a time of great social change and turmoil. The cultural and religious landscape was in flux. Although both men would become spiritual giants of their age activating incredible religious movements, neither one sat back in the quiet of their offices and plotted such an eventuality. At first, they found themselves displaced by the chaos all around them. Initially, they were not attempting to create an answer or response to the challenges of a society in chaos and change; they were simply trying to personally survive. The beginning point of God's hand in their lives starts with their personal dislocation brought on by chaotic times. This withdrawal, this exile, is what creates prophets and prophetic teaching, as Bruce Gordon notes of Calvin's life:

> Exile had been the fate of the prophets and of David fleeing Saul; it was
> now Calvin's lot. From his conversion experience he had undergone

> *a spiritual journey which led to the gradual break with the Catholic Church. There was a no defining or dramatic moment; it took place in study, conversation and prayer—all of which remain hidden from the eyes of historians. Exile was an act of obedience to God, a separation from a false church and a declaration of faith. The role of the prophet was as an outsider, and to respond to God's call in his conversion Calvin had had to leave France.*[4]

Gordon writes of a slow, almost unseen exile, a dislocation from what is known that happens almost unconsciously. This dislocation creates a distance between us and what is known and comfortable. This exile creates a constant state of not feeling at home. No longer is it possible to fall into a state of blissful contentment, in which we do not examine the world. The exile is constantly reminded of how the things around them are not what they should be.

Those of us who lead and believe in a time of spiritual ghostliness feel this dislocation all around us. It is the discomfort of feeling a great distance between the vision of the kingdom and the direction of the culture we live in. It is the hurt as friends leave active faith or faith altogether and disappear into the beautiful apocalypse. It is the relentless pressure that pastors, leaders, and disciples face as we call people to submission and worship of God in a culture of seduction and pleasure. In the presence of such pressure, we have before us two options. First, we can become bitterer, more despondent, more isolated. We understand the situation we face and we flounder in the face of the challenge. Second, we can simply attempt to lessen the pressure by shaping our theology, spirituality, and lifestyle to suit the dogma of the surrounding culture.

We lessen the pressure by surgically removing those parts of our faith that clash with the mode of the day. For Calvin this was a very real option. With his world-class intellect, a career as a leading French humanist intellectual in Paris—the global capital of academic study—was a real possibility. But there was a problem. Inside of him, the conviction toward the Word of God was leading him into the Protestantism that was sweeping the Continent. Many around Calvin shared such convictions, and simply kept quiet about them for fear of persecution, going about life as kinds of crypto-Protestants.

Calvin could not take such a path. Instead he allowed himself to be swept into the waters of exile, and to be shaped into the prophetic mold that God can use exile to sculpt. The same choice is before us. The challenge of this book is to allow the unique pressure that we face, alongside submitting to God, to forge within us a prophetic posture.

2) BREAK FROM CULTURAL NARRATIVES

Distance from the prevailing culture enables one to examine and recognize cultural myths and blind spots.

While Calvin's exile would lead him to Geneva, Ignatius's wanderings would land him in the small Spanish town of Manresa. It was not a place that he had intended to stay more than a few days, but a combination of illness and deep experiences with God would ensure that Ignatius remained in the town for a year. Within this small town, he retreated to a cave, in which he would spend countless hours in prayer. Ignatius was a man who had all the trappings of worldly success. He was a consummate soldier, a charming courtier, skilled in the social graces of his day. He had all of the requirements for a life of secular success. In the cave in Manresa, through isolation, prayer, and illness, God would break the cultural narratives that had formed in him. Ignatius would swap his ideas of worldly success for total submission to God. The distance that injury, illness, and spiritual isolation had brought him allowed him to gain distance from the power of the forming cultural narratives around him. Before he could lead, before he could minister, before he could influence, he must first orientate himself primarily around dependence upon God.

God did not press a reset button on Ignatius or Calvin, causing them to in a moment lose all that had formed them as individuals up until the point of their withdrawal and encounter with God. Ignatius's military background would influence the discipline and order he would establish in his ministry, the Jesuits. The political skills he learned as he hung around the edges of courtly life would enable him to engage with key political and royal leaders as his Jesuit order grew. Calvin's intellectual training in academia and the discipline of study he had learned since a youth would greatly aid his writing of significantly influential theology.

This is what the great student of Christian leadership Bobby Clinton labels "sovereign foundations." Sovereign foundations are, according to Clinton, the way that "God providentially works through family, environment, and historical events."[5] (Clinton notes that it is often not till later that we recognize the importance of these sovereign foundations.) Instead of wiping us clean of these influences, the process of withdrawal enables us to see for what they are the false narratives that have driven our lives, and it compels us to make a break from them. This break is both a yes and a no: a yes to the process that God is calling us to, and a no to the false narrative. For Ignatius "had made the 'grand refusal,' which was equally the grand acceptance, and the whole trend of his affections changed with a swift completion possible only to a soul at once so eager and decisive."[6] Ignatius, like anyone who has allowed God to take them through the Withdraw/Return process, was now free of the false narrative that had kept him enchained and able to dedicate himself to God's plan for his life.

3) SELF-INSIGHT INTO ONE'S FLAWS

After identifying the myths of the dominant culture, withdrawal enables one to identify personal flaws. To examine the way in which the individual has bought into the culture myths themselves.

Reflecting upon Ignatius's time at Manresa, Chris Lowney discerns that alongside the deep communion with God and the break with the false narrative of his past, he gained something else: "He walked away with deep self-understanding, able to pinpoint his flaws with greater maturity and accuracy than ever before."[7]

Ignatius now clearly saw himself, his own flaws, his own sinfulness. Lowney notes that this self-insight into one's flaws was crucial to his coming leadership. Ignatius was discovering that the starting point for ministry and spiritual influence begins in true humility, in understanding our own wretchedness. Calvin also understood this principle, counseling in his commentary on the book of Philippians, "For however anyone may have outstanding endowments, he should consider that they have not been given to him that he might be self-complacent, that he might exalt himself or even venerate himself. Let him instead work at correcting and detecting his faults, and he will have great material for humility."[8]

In isolation, exile, and withdrawal, God enables us to grasp our own flaws and fallenness. The disciple who wishes to influence others, yet is unaware of his or her own flaws, has the potential to do much harm.

Self-insight into our personal flaws enables us to also see clearly the way in which false cultural narratives have shaped our personal lives. After recognizing the false narratives, after making a cognitive recognition of their influence on those around us, we must fearlessly look upon the way in which our emotional, spiritual, and social lives have been shaped by them.

4) CONVERSION EXPERIENCE INTO ABIDING

Having identified and rejected the dominant cultural myths, having identified personal flaws, the individual is invited to a deep and abiding relationship with God.

Both Calvin and Ignatius before their experience of withdrawal were undoubtedly already believers in Christ. During their withdrawal, both experienced a kind of conversion, not into salvation but into a deeper communion with Christ. Chris Lowney notes that not only did Ignatius emerge from his withdrawal at Manresa with a clear insight into his flaws, he gained also at the same time the ability "to appreciate himself as a uniquely dignified and gifted person in a world that seemed far more positive than it did when he entered Manresa."[9]

This insight arose from a deeper intimacy with God. While in the cave at Manresa, Ignatius prayerfully read through the gospel of Jesus multiple times, meditating in particular upon Jesus' saving death on the cross. Ignatius emerged with a profound knowledge of God's immense love for him. This is where his new insight into his giftedness and dignity emerged from. These things were given to him as gifts of God. They were not the work of his hand but rather of the Creator. Before Ignatius entered Manresa, he would have been aware of Jesus' love, but now he knew it at a profoundly deep level.

In the conversion experience into abiding, we are invited beyond knowledge into spiritual knowledge. We are invited into a new mode of living, one marked by a deep and constant communion with God. False cultural narratives tempt us to find success elsewhere apart from God's design; they encourage us to empower ourselves with sources apart from God. Having been withdrawn, broken from the false narrative, and gaining insight into our own flaws, we are invited to move from striving in our own power to abiding in God's strength.

5) A MESSAGE THAT CONNECTS

The experience of withdrawal. The identification of cultural myths, and a conversion into an abiding relationship with God, enables the individual to develop orthodox teachings that carry deep resonance.

Calvin was a refugee fleeing religious persecution. This reality dominated his life. He was also one of countless others across Europe who were experiencing a similar fate. As he led and ministered in Geneva, religious refugees would pour in from France fleeing persecution. Inevitably as refugees the world over understand, in such a situation it is not long before the displeasure of the host community is felt. While the Genevans and the French refugees shared a common creed of Protestantism, their experience could not have been further apart. The refugees had lost their homes, their possessions, and their livelihoods. Many had suffered the heartbreaking experience of relational breakdown, as religious conflict split families and friendships in two.

The cultural condition surrounding Calvin, written on the faces of the refugees who listened to his sermons, was one of exile. It was a palpable yearning for a home to which they could never return. Calvin could recognize this yearning because it was his own. The language of exile, of yearning for home, began to enter Calvin's teaching. "Calvin set out a theme that he would continue to develop throughout his life—the Christian life as pilgrimage through the world toward eternity. Drawing on his own experience, though never referring to himself, he offered comfort to those who suffer for their faith in God's Word by holding before the reader the examples of great figures of the Bible, such as Job and Abraham,"[10] writes Gordon. Elements of the Withdraw/Return process were now falling into place.

Calvin's own experience of withdrawal through exile enabled him to understand and speak into the exile experience. His abiding relationship with God and his deep reading of Scripture enabled him to speak into the cultural experience of those around him. He was able to connect the biblical themes of exile, sojourning, and home with the cultural experience of exile and the yearning for home in those to whom he was ministering. Because of the prophetic voice that had been born in him due to his own exile, Calvin was able to undercut the false cultural narrative that refugees would naturally feel, that is, belief that their yearning for home would end when they returned to their abodes or comfortably established a new residence. The true home of the believer was heaven.

Jesus, rather than a hospitable king or republic who offered asylum, was their true hope. Calvin's own experience as a refugee enabled him to speak into the cultural condition of fellow refugees. Calvin's abiding relationship with Christ and his drenching himself in God's Word enabled him to point those around him to their true hope. This is what I describe as a cultural key. Calvin had not changed his orthodoxy in the face of a changed and challenging cultural situation. Rather, he had dug deeper into orthodoxy to find revelation that not only answered the questions of the day, but pushed further beyond them into the eternal.

Through the process of withdrawal we gain distance from false cultural narratives. When we gain insight into our own flaws, we see how the false cultural narrative affects an individual. Through deepened abiding with God and meditating upon His Word, we see both spiritual roots of a false narrative and its positive biblical alternative. A cultural key is a powerful insight that acts as a ministry tool to unlock the door to an area of ministry in which fruitfulness has been difficult.

6) RETURN TO EQUIP OTHERS

Armed with a cultural key, the individual returns to minister to those within the dominant culture.

Ignatius was profoundly changed at Manresa. He had been taken by God into a deeper communion with Him. Having experienced such a great spiritual transformation through being withdrawn by God, Ignatius could have simply moved on, enjoying his deepening walk by himself. Or he could have joined one of the monasteries around Manresa in order to try and sustain the spiritual experience.

God, however, had other plans. Ignatius's experience was not just for him to enjoy; rather it was something that had to be passed on to others. Reflecting upon his own experience of withdrawal and deepening with God, Ignatius devised what came to be known as his spiritual exercises. The exercises were a kind of workbook, informed by Ignatius's own experiences, which guided others through their own process of withdrawal and deepening. The book would go on to be one of the most read Christian books in history, guiding countless others into a deepening relationship with God. Ignatius could not stay in the cave at Manresa forever. He had to return to the world outside, and his spiritual exercises were a powerful fruit born of that return.

Calvin wrote, "While my one great object was to live in seclusion without being known, God so led me about through different turnings and change that he never permitted me to rest in any place, until, in spite of my natural disposition, he brought me forth to public notice."[11] Calvin's exile led him into a place of influence and leadership, and his *Institutes* like Ignatius's *Exercises* would become a Christian classic. These works would act as kinds of artifacts of the Withdraw/Return process, works that would open up entire new worlds for countless others.

Both men would produce not just books but also disciples. Ignatius would found his Company of Jesus, the Jesuits. The ten men he would pour himself into would go on to serve and minister across the world, spreading Christianity into places as far away as India, Japan, and China. Calvin would also pour himself into scores of pastors and leaders, as he built not just a church, but a vision of the church founded on the New Testament. These movements would shape scores of individuals, movements, institutions, and whole cultures.

Going Beyond the Culture of the Ghost

Shaken to their cores by the events of the crucifixion, Jesus' disciples are gathered when suddenly the risen Lord appears in their midst. "Peace be with you." They thought He was a ghost and were frightened. And they were right to be afraid of a ghost. For the appearance of a genuine ghost runs contrary to what the gospel teaches us. A ghost is a disembodied spirit, shorn of its body. It inhabits a half-world, in between the material and supernatural. It is a floating half-memory of a life that has passed. The appearance of Jesus' disembodied spirit would no doubt be unnerving, but more importantly it would be a devastating confirmation of His death.

Yet in Luke's gospel something deeper is at play: Jesus is not a ghost. He said to them, "Why are you troubled, and why do doubts rise in your minds? Look at my hands and my feet. It is I myself! Touch me and see; a ghost does not have flesh and bones, as you see I have" (Luke 24:38–39 NIV). This is not the appearance of a disembodied spirit whose business is haunting. Jesus is not just spirit, but also body. He has flesh and bone. His invitation to the disciples is to look upon Him, to touch Him, to viscerally feel their skin upon His skin and touch God's salvation history as it breaks into the world in real time.

Jesus is otherworldly, but He is not from nor heading toward Hades, Sheol, or any other resting place for the dead. The world to which He will go is heaven, where He will be seated at the right hand of God. This human body, with hair, skin, bones, and importantly scars, will have dominion over the universe. "He . . . who ascended higher than all the heavens, in order to fill the whole universe" (Ephesians 4:10 NIV) asks for a bite to eat. The living God, Christ risen, appears and asks for a snack.

Such a scene could at first seem like a piece of irreverent comedy inserted in the gospel narrative. It is however crucial to what Jesus is teaching the disciples. Jesus then takes a piece of roasted fish and begins to eat. This is resurrection in all its mysterious glory. "And he took it [the fish] and ate it in their presence" (Luke 24:43 NIV). Jesus is solid; He is flesh and bones. His body is more solid, permanent, and concrete than the bodies of the disciples who watch His chewing jaw in "joy and amazement" (v. 41 NIV). They will pass and the worm will eat of their bodies. But Jesus' post-resurrection body will never fade. It is stout and corporeal, yet radiating God's eternal glory.

Pressing home the point, Jesus says, "'This is what I told you while I was still with you. Everything must be fulfilled that is written about me in the Law of Moses, the Prophets and the Psalms.'" Then He opened their minds so they could understand the Scriptures. He told them, "'This is what is written: The Messiah will suffer and rise from the dead on the third day, and repentance for the forgiveness of sins will be preached in his name to all nations, beginning at Jerusalem. You are my witnesses of these things. I am going to send you what my Father has promised; but stay in the city until you have been clothed with power from on high'" (Luke 24:44–49 NIV).

Jesus' death and resurrection are God's breaking into history, His righting of all wrongs. These are the days that the prophets hoped for, and Jesus points out the salvation history that He is now fulfilling, a salvation history that reaches back to undo humanity's rebellion against God. This is the ultimate Withdraw/Return, written large on a cosmic scale. Jesus has passed into death and come back. He has been cursed with the sin of humankind yet returns radiant with glory, having defeated sin. Now pulsating resurrection reality, Jesus returns from withdraw with saving knowledge.

The disciples, so often misunderstanding and confused, now get it. The two disciples on the road to Emmaus find their eyes opened and recognize the risen Jesus as He expounds the Scriptures pointing toward Himself. The scales fall as He breaks bread with them, pointing to the way that Christ will speak through the church, opening eyes and hearts through word and bread. After His death the resurrected Christ appeared "to them during 40 days and speaking about the kingdom of God" (Acts 1:3). With their minds opened by Christ, the disciples are now filled with worship. They now understand the tectonic, cosmic plates that have been shifting underneath their feet.

Everything has changed. The resurrection transformation that Jesus has gone through begins to transform the disciples. When Jesus needed them most, they disappeared. Their embryonic faith is filled with fear, the belief with doubt. When Jesus needs them in the garden, they are not present and awake but asleep. When His execution comes, they vanish like ghosts. Yet upon His return from the dead, the often bumbling, doubting, sometimes power-hungry disciples morph into solid, devoted apostles; sent ones, the gold standard of Jesus' teachings. A solid creative minority has been birthed which will shake the world.

Before His death and resurrection, watching Jesus' ministry from afar one would have to question His wisdom and intelligence in entrusting His mission, ministry, and future legacy to such an unimpressive group of disciples. Jesus had the ability to gather a crowd through His communication gifts, and miraculous signs and wonders. Yet He would often deliver parables to the crowds while saving the cream of His teaching for His small band of disciples. After gathering such a following, after gaining such a platform, why hold back from the masses to seemingly waste your best material on a group of men who often get it all wrong anyway? What is Jesus' problem with crowds? Why is He always running from them? Why is He always in retreat?

We can see the answer to the questions and understand Jesus' strategy of ministry when we examine His first leadership withdrawal. After His public baptism, Jesus initiates a practice that He will repeat during His ministry: He retreats to an isolated marginal place. We like Jesus find ourselves in a desert. The desert for Jesus must have been incredibly lonely, in ways that we as contemporary individualists cannot image. Life in the first century was a constant rubbing of shoulders. It was intense community; everyone knew everyone's business, and everyone watched out for each other. It was also an intensely religious life, filled with all of the rituals and institutions of Judaism.

Torah observance meant that everything pointed back to God; your choice of meal, of clothing, all presented you with a choice to commit, to again choose to follow God. The study of Scripture and the synagogue were central to community life, occupying the place that television, the Internet, and media fill in ours. At night, the air would have echoed with prayers and sung psalms. It was a place without an inch of secularity. Drenched in, embodied, committed faith.

Yet in the desert, nothing or no one. No community, no communal faith, no enfleshed worship, no relationships or responsibility. Jesus experiences the atomization and aloneness feared by humans throughout history, but embraced as normal in our age, today in our desert, shorn of embodied faith, of institutions. Meaning, tradition, community deconstructed and degraded. Like Jesus, the worshiping community of faith that once surrounded us has now disappeared. Into the now vacant space, into this desert of faith, just as he did with Jesus, the devil comes. To Jesus, he offered shortcuts to success, strategies for the spectacular. He offers a chance to go visible fast, and to choose surface over depth.

The evil one offers Jesus an alternate ministry strategy. He tempts Him to throw Himself off the temple, in a faux-suicide attempt in which the devil promises that God will intervene with the deployment of angels. Satan is effectively encouraging Jesus to launch His ministry in the most public of places, the temple complex, ground zero of Israel's religious scene, with a spectacular and undeniable miracle. Such a miracle would no doubt incite pandemonium, and the most recalcitrant of Pharisee, the most cynical Sadducee, the most bloody-minded Zealot would be wowed. Instantaneously, a crowd would gather hailing the arrival of the messianic King. No traipsing through the Judean countryside, no endless sermons, no never-ending requests for healing, no opposition, no threats of blasphemy, no debates with scholars. In a flash, the instant platform of a flashmob. In the space of seconds He would have adulation and followers. He would have a crowd. But Jesus did not need to win public opinion; He needed disciples, ones who had faith and devotion, and who saw the scope of salvation history, rather than being wowed for an instant. Jesus' plan to redeem the world was founded on discipling, trusting, and handing over His ministry to a small group of trusted followers and friends. Jesus invested in the few to change the many. He went deep to go wide.

> JESUS INVESTED IN THE FEW TO CHANGE THE MANY.

To do this, however, He needed disciples who could learn to abide in the Father rather than listen to the competing claims for truth surrounding them. Jesus' three-year ministry was a public affair, announcing the kingdom and making His way to the miracle of the cross, but it also was an investment in the discipleship community that had gathered around Him. This three-year preparation consisted of Jesus modeling the kingdom way of life, of teaching them the good news of God, of sending them out to learn on the job. They were the foundation upon which He would build His church; His intent was for them to be the incarnation of His mission in the world, the heralds of the gospel sent into the world. Jesus knew that opposition would come, that the pressure upon the disciples would be immense. He told them that to follow Him, they too must take up their crosses. He was creating extremeophile disciples.

The essential message that Jesus taught the disciples is captured in an exchange between Jesus and His disciples in John's gospel. It is the Last Supper, and Judas has left the meal to betray his Lord. Jesus tells His disciples, "Children, I am with you a little while longer. You will look for Me, and just as I told the Jews, 'Where I am going you cannot come'" (John 13:33). Peter, Philip, and Judas the son of James, concerned at Jesus' impending departure, ask a series of questions. Jesus delivers a series of teachings in response to their questions and concerns. This is the heart of His message:

> Remain in Me, and I in you. Just as a branch is unable to produce fruit by itself unless it remains on the vine, so neither can you unless you remain in Me. I am the vine, you are the branches. The one who remains in Me and I in him produces much fruit, because you can do nothing without Me. (John 15:4–5)

The only way to be truly alive, to produce fruit, spiritual fruit that lasts into eternity, is to remain in Christ. To be unable to produce fruit that lasts is tragic. Jesus asked that the disciples now abide in Him, the way that He had modeled abiding in His Father. The pattern of withdrawing to engage that Jesus had shown through His ministry, He would now ask of His disciples. The fleshly parts of them that wished for glory, for more immediate results, that doubted, that feared, now must be changed by abiding in the Father. In the same way, our task is to teach those whom God has placed in our charge to abide in Him.

To do this in our context of the beautiful world, the inner, private world, tempted and corroded by the promises of our culture of seduction, we must again learn to abide in the Father. Building our public profile is always a much easier task; it is measurable and tangible. Leading people to allow God to rebuild their ghostly and fragile inner selves is a much more nuanced task. To learn to abide in Christ, we also must break from the lures that surround us, while still offering good news to the culture that seduces us. The process of Withdraw/Return is used by God to do precisely this. Throughout history we see this process in the lives of His great saints and witnesses—the creative minorities who have clung unashamedly to their faith in Christ, while bringing the gospel of the God who gave His life and His kingdom blessing to the wider culture.

Notes

INTRODUCTION

1. Michael Gove, "Why I'm Proud to Be a Christian (and Jeremy Paxman Should Be Ashamed)," *The Spectator*, April 4, 2015, http://www.spectator.co.uk/featu res/9487882/in-defence-of-christianity.

2. Go on Choosing God: A Q&A with Scot McKnight, http://www.patheos.com/ Books/Book-Club/Scot-McKnight-A-Long-Faithfulness/QA-061515.html.

CHAPTER 1 – OUR CURRENT POST-CHRISTIANITY

1. Henri de Lubac, *The Drama of Atheist Humanism* (San Francisco: Ignatius, 1995), 70.

2. David Brooks, "It's Not about You," *The New York Times*, May 30, 2011, http://www.nytimes.com/2011/05/31/opinion/31brooks.html?_r=0.

3. Mark Lilla, "The Truth about Our Libertarian Age: Why the dogma of democracy doesn't always make the world better," *The New Republic*, June 17, 2014, http://www.newrepublic.com/article/118043/our-libertarian-age-dog ma-democracy-dogma-decline.

4. Andrew Keen, *The Internet Is Not the Answer* (London: Atlantic, 2015), 214.

5. Malcolm Muggeridge, *Conversion: A Spiritual Journey* (London: Collins, 1988).

6. Eric Voegelin, *Science, Politics and Gnosticism: Two Essays* (Washington DC: Regnery, 1968), 64.

7. Joseph Bottum, *An Anxious Age: The Post-Protestant Ethic and the Spirit of America* (New York: Image, 2014), 15.

8. See James K. A. Smith, *How (Not) to Be Secular: Reading Charles Taylor* (Grand Rapids: Eerdmans, 2014), 139.

9. Peter Brown, *Augustine of Hippo: A Biography* (Berkeley, CA: University of California Press, 1969).

CHAPTER 2 – THE HISTORY OF "RELEVANT"

1. Christopher Lasch, *The Culture of Narcissism: American Life in an Age of Diminishing Expectations* (New York: Warner, 1980), 14.

2. For more on the Nine O'Clock Service see Roland Howard, *The Rise and Fall of the Nine O'Clock Service: A Cult within the Church?* (London: Continuum-3PL, 1996).

3. See Timotheus Vermeulen and Robin van den Akker, "Notes on Metamodernism," *Journal of Aesthetics & Culture 2010*, http://www.aestheticsandculture.net/index.php/jac/article/view/5677/6306.

CHAPTER 3 – HOW MUCH MORE RELEVANT CAN WE GET?

1. Quoted in Niall Ferguson, *Civilization: The Six Killer Apps of Western Power* (London: Penguin, 2011), 257.

2. Quoted in Michael Burleigh, *Sacred Causes: Religion and Politics from the European Dictators to Al Qaeda* (London: Harper Perennial, 2006), 475.

3. Ibid., 474.

4. See Philip Rieff, *My Life among the Deathworks: Illustrations of the Aesthetics of Authority* (Charlottesville, VA: University of Virginia Press, 2006).

5. Ibid., 138.

6. See Evgeny Morozov, *To Save Everything, Click Here: The Folly of Technological Solutionism* (New York: Public Affairs, 2014).

7. Jonathan Sacks, "On Creative Minorities," *First Things*, January 2014, http://www.firstthings.com/article/2014/01/on-creative-minorities.

8. Ibid.

9. Ibid.

10. See Arnold J. Toynbee, *A Study of History* (London: Oxford University Press, 1946).

11. Sacks, "On Creative Minorities."

12. Ibid.

13. See Martin Buber, *Eclipse of God: Studies in the Relation between Religion and Philosophy* (New York: Harper & Row, 1952).

CHAPTER 4 – THE GOSPEL OF SELF (GNOSTICISM)

1. David Bentley Hart, *In the Aftermath: Provocations and Laments* (Grand Rapids: Eerdmans, 2009), 17.

2. Ibid., 15.

3. Tom Wolfe, "The Me Decade and the Third Awakening," *New York Magazine*, August 23, 1976.

4. Roger Lundin, *The Culture of Interpretation: Christian Faith and the Postmodern World* (Grand Rapids: Eerdmans, 1993), 77–78.

5. Ross Douthat, *Bad Religion: How We Became a Nation of Heretics* (New York: Simon & Schuster, 2012), 3.

6. Hans Urs von Balthasar, *The Scandal of the Incarnation: Irenaeus against the Heresies* (San Francisco: Ignatius Press, 1990), 4.

7. For more on Jung's Gnostic influences see chapter 7 of Gary Lachman, *Jung The Mystic: The Esoteric Dimensions of Carl Jung's Life and Teachings* (New York: Penguin, 2010).

8. See Jessica Grogan, *Encountering America: Humanistic Psychology, Sixties Culture and the Shaping of the Modern Self* (New York: Harper Perennial, 2013), 19.

9. Harold Bloom, *The American Religion: The Emergence of the Post-Christian Religion* (New York: Simon & Schuster, 1991).

10. Ibid., 263.

11. Christian Smith and Melinda Lundquist Denton, *Soul Searching: The Religious and Spiritual Lives of American Teenagers* (New York: Oxford University Press USA, 2009), 162–63.

CHAPTER 5 – AN EXCITING OPPORTUNITY

1. John Wolffe, *The Expansion of Evangelicalism: The Age of Wilberforce, More, Chalmers and Finney* (Nottingham, UK: InterVarsity Press, 2006), 40–41.

2. See Richard Foster, *Celebration of Discipline: The Path to Spiritual Growth* (San Francisco: HarperSanFrancisco, 2002).

3. See Margaret J. Wheatley, *Leadership and the New Science: Discovering Order in a Chaotic World* (Oakland, CA: Berrett-Koehler Publishers, 2006).

4. Warren I. Susman, *Culture as History: The Transformation of American Society in the Twentieth Century* (New York: Pantheon, 1973), 272.

5. Thomas Molnar, *Authority and Its Enemies* (New Rochelle, NY: Arlington House, 1976), 9.

Chapter 6 – Reject the Implicit Prosperity Gospel. We Are Slaves, not Seekers.

1. See N. T. Wright, *How God Became King: The Forgotten Story of the Gospels* (New York: HarperCollins, 2012).

2. Adam B. Seligman, *Modernity's Wager: Authority, the Self, and Transcendence* (Princeton, NJ: Princeton University Press, 2000), 3.

3. David T. Koyzis, *We Answer to Another: Authority, Office, and the Image of God* (Eugene, OR: Pickwick, 2014), 12.

4. See Robert Wuthnow, *After Heaven: Spirituality in America Since the 1950s* (Berkeley, CA: University of California Press, 1998).

5. Cyril O'Regan, *Gnostic Return in Modernity* (Albany, NY: State University of New York Press, 2001), 17.

6. Quoted in "Waugh vs. Hollywood," in the *Guardian*, May 22, 2004, http://www.theguardian.com/film/2004/may/22/classics.film.

7. Gilles Lipovetsky, *Hypermodern Times* (Cambridge, UK: Polity, 2005), 53.

8. Ibid., 55.

9. Ibid., 55–56.

10. See Ulrich Beck, *Risk Society: Towards a New Modernity* (Thousand Oaks, CA: Sage, 1992).

11. See Frank Furedi, *Culture of Fear Revisited: Risk-Taking and the Morality of Low Expectation* (London: Continuum, 2006).

12. Lipovetsky, *Hypermodern Times*, 61.

Chapter 7 – Stop Catering to "Public" Opinion

1. Michael Burleigh, *Earthly Powers: Religion and Politics in Europe from the Enlightenment to the Great War* (London: Harper Perennial, 2005), 7.

2. Marina Benjamin, *Living at the End of the World* (London: Picador, 1998), 20.

3. Peter Augustine Lawler, *Aliens in America: The Strange Truth about Our Souls* (Wilmington, DE: ISI, 2002), 80.

4. Allan Bloom, *The Closing of the American Mind: How Higher Education Has Failed Democracy and Impoverished the Souls of Today's Students* (New York: Simon & Schuster, 1987), 155.

5. Richard John Neuhaus, *American Babylon: Notes of a Christian Exile* (New York: Basic, 2009), 161–162.

6. Christopher Shannon, *Conspicuous Criticism: Tradition, the Individual, and Culture in American Social Thought, from Veblen to Mills* (Baltimore, MD: Johns Hopkins University Press, 1996), 176.

7. Ibid.

8. Richard Rorty and Gianni Vattimo, ed. Santiago Zabala, *The Future of Religion* (New York: Columbia University Press, 2005), 40.

9. Jaron Lanier, *You Are Not a Gadget: A Manifesto* (New York: Vintage, 2010), 53.

10. Zygmunt Bauman, *Culture in a Liquid Modern World* (Cambridge, UK: Polity, 2011), 13, 17.

11. Thomas Bergler, *The Juvenilization of American Christianity* (Grand Rapids: Eerdmans, 2012), 11.

12. Tom Wright, *Creation, Power and Truth: The Gospel in a World of Cultural Confusion* (London: SPCK, 2013), 36.

13. See James K. A. Smith, *How (Not) to Be Secular: Reading Charles Taylor* (Grand Rapids: Eerdmans, 2014), 49.

14. C. S. Lewis, *Mere Christianity* (New York: Macmillan, 1952), 134.

15. Hans Boersma, *Heavenly Participation: The Weaving of a Sacramental Tapestry* (Grand Rapids: Eerdmans, 2011), 45.

16. Lewis, *Mere Christianity*, 135.

17. "To See Things as They Are: A Response to Michael Hanby," George Weigel, *First Things*, February 2015, http://www.firstthings.com/article/2015/02/to-see-things-as-they-are.

18. Hans Urs von Balthasar, *The Scandal of the Incarnation: Irenaeus against the Heresies* (San Francisco: Ignatius Press, 1990), 13.

19. Alexander Schmemann, *For the Life of the World: Sacraments and Orthodoxy* (Crestwood, NY: St. Vladimir's Seminary Press, 1963), 35.

CHAPTER 8 – DON'T OFFER EVERYTHING. DELIVER TRUTH.

1. See "The Bureaucracy of Terror: New Secret Documents Reveal al Qaeda's Real Challenges," Jennifer R. Williams, *Foreign Affairs*, March 25, 2015, https://www.foreignaffairs.com/articles/2015-03-25/bureaucracy-terror.

2. Moisés Naim, *The End of Power: From Boardrooms to Battlefields and Churches to States, Why Being in Charge Isn't What It Used to Be* (New York: Basic, 2013), 25.

3. See Philip Rieff, *The Triumph of the Therapeutic: Uses of Faith after Freud* (New York: Harper Torchbooks, 1966).

4. "Al-Qaida 'cut off and ripped apart by Isis.'" Spencer Ackerman, Shiv Malik, Ali Younes, Mustafa Khalili, *The Guardian*, June 11, 2015, http://www.theguardian.com/world/2015/jun/10/isis-onslaught-has-broken-al-qaida-its-spiritual-leaders-admit.

5. Naim, *End of Power*, 24.

6. See Daniel Yankelovich, *New Rules: Searching for Self-Fulfillment in a World Turned Upside Down* (New York: Bantam, 1981), 56.

7. Søren Kierkegaard, *The Present Age: On the Death of Rebellion* (New York: Harper Perennial, 1962).

8. Ibid., 33–34.

9. Eugene Peterson, *Run with the Horses: The Quest for Life at Its Best* (Downers Grove, IL: InterVarsity Press, 1985).

10. Kierkegaard, *Present Age*, 33–34.

11. Ibid., 35.

12. I am not decrying or arguing against the need for a public theology altogether. Rather, I am attempting to point out that Christians, and evangelicals in particular, are overly obsessed with what the phantom public thinks of us.

13. Gordon MacDonald, *Mid-Course Correction: Re-Ordering Your Private World for the Next Part of Your Journey* (Nashville: Thomas Nelson, 2000), 24.

14. Christopher Dawson, *Religion and the Rise of Western Culture* (New York: Doubleday, 1950), 53–54.

CHAPTER 9 – RE-CREATE THE INSTITUTION

1. Grace Davie, *Religion in Modern Europe: A Memory Mutates* (Oxford, UK: Oxford University Press, 2000), 33.

2. Damian Thompson in "2067: the End of British Christianity," in *The Spectator*, June 13, 2015. http://www.spectator.co.uk/features/9555222/2067-the-end-of-british-christianity/.

3. Alister E. McGrath, *Heresy: A History of Defending the Truth* (New York: HarperOne, 2009), 122–123.

4. Philip J. Lee, *Against the Protestant Gnostics* (New York: Oxford University Press, 1987), 33.

5. Ibid.

6. Kurt Rudolph, *Gnosis: The Nature and History of Gnosticism* (San Francisco: HarperSanFrancisco, 1987), 218.

7. George Packer, *The Unwinding: An Inner History of the New America* (New York: Farrar, Strauss and Giroux, 2013), 34.

8. Robert Putnam, *Bowling Alone: The Collapse and Revival of American Community* (New York: Simon & Schuster, 2000), 16.

9. Daron Acemoglu and James Robinson, *Why Nations Fail: The Origins of Power, Prosperity and Poverty* (London: Profile, 2012).

10. See Niall Ferguson, *The Great Degeneration: How Institutions Decay and Economies Die* (London: Allen Lane, 2012).

11. Malcolm Gladwell, "Small Change: Why the Revolution Will Not Be Tweeted," *The New Yorker*, October 4, 2010, http://www.newyorker.com/magazine/2010/10/04/small-change-malcolm-gladwell.

12. Ray Ortlund, "Is Your Church an Institution?" The Gospel Coalition, December 11, 2012, http://www.thegospelcoalition.org/blogs/rayortlund/2012/12/11/is-your-church-institution/.

13. This is known as the *Gemeinschaft* and *Gesellschaft* dichotomy, also explored by Max Weber.

14. Thomas F. Torrance, *Incarnation: The Person and Life of Christ* (Milton Keynes, UK: Paternoster, 2008), 42.

15. Robert A. Nisbet, *Tradition and Revolt: Historical and Sociological Essays* (New York: Random House, 1968), see chapter 7, "Moral Values and Community."

16. "Saved by Tsunami Folklore," BBC News, March 10, 2007, http://news.bbc.co.uk/2/hi/programmes/from_our_own_correspondent/6435979.stm.

17. Andy Crouch, *Playing God: Redeeming the Gift of Power* (Downers Grove, IL: InterVarsity Press, 2013), 188.

18. Ruth Haley Barton, *Strengthening the Soul of Your Leadership: Seeking God in the Crucible of Ministry* (Grand Rapids: InterVarsity Press, 2008), 108.

19. Ibid., 111.

20. Ibid., 112.

21. See Todd D. Hunter, *Giving Church Another Chance: Finding New Meaning in Spiritual Practices* (Downers Grove, IL: InterVarsity Press, 2010), in particular pages 27–38, to understand the shift from seeing church as something to consume to a spiritual practice to bless others.

22. Ronald Rolheiser, *The Holy Longing: The Search for a Christian Spirituality* (New York: Image, 1998), 69.

23. Malcolm Gladwell, *David and Goliath: Underdogs, Misfits, and the Art of Battling Giants* (New York: Little, Brown, and Company, 2013), 36.

24. Scott Anderson, *Lawrence of Arabia: War, Deceit, Imperial Folly and the Making of the Modern Middle East* (London: Atlantic, 2013), 3.

25. See Roger Scruton, *The Face of God: The Gifford Lectures* (London: Bloomsbury, 2012).

26. See Rodney Stark, *The Rise of Christianity: A Sociologist Reconsiders History* (Princeton, NJ: Princeton University Press, 1996).

Chapter 10 – Withdraw/Return

1. Daniel Goleman, *Focus: The Hidden Driver of Excellence* (London: Bloomsbury, 2013), 33.

2. Andrew Zolli and Ann Marie Healy, *Resilience: In Times of Upheaval Why Do Some People, Communities, Companies and Systems Recover, Persists and Thrive, While Others Fall Apart?* (London: Headline, 2012), 8.

3. See Arnold J. Toynbee, *A Study of History* (London: Oxford University Press, 1946).

4. Bruce Gordon, *Calvin* (New Haven, CT: Yale University Press, 2009), 42.

5. J. Robert Clinton, *The Making of a Leader: Recognizing the Lessons and Stages of Leadership Development* (Colorado Springs: NavPress, 1988), 44.

6. Francis Thompson, *St. Ignatius Loyola* (London: Universe, 1962), 7.

7. Chris Lowney, *Heroic Leadership: Best Practices from a 450-Year-Old Company That Changed the World* (Chicago: Loyola Press, 2003), 45.

8. Quoted in Gordon, *Calvin*, 111.

9. Lowney, *Heroic Leadership*, 45.

10. Gordon, *Calvin*, 44.

11. Quoted in Gordon, *Calvin*, 47.

Acknowledgments

Thanks to the team at Moody; Randall, Natalie, Parker, Betsey. Thanks to Trudi and my family for their understanding during the writing process. Thanks to my parents, Garry and Joy, for letting me use their front room to write. Thanks to Sarah, Melody, and Glen for reading drafts and offering advice. Thanks to Red Church for all their support and understanding. I am eternally grateful to those who prayed for me during the writing. Most of all thanks to God for all that He gives.